INSPIRED WORD

A Christian Devotional

John Thomas Jr.

Inspired Word

ISBN: 978-0-615-96301-3

DEDICATION

To all who poured into my life knowing &
unknowingly.

PROLOGUE

In the year of 2007 I had a friend that was a big-time club promoter. His main club night was on Thursday nights. He always invited me out to his events and I would go most of the time to hangout, but I would counter by texting him an invite to church. In addition, I would text him what I call my "Daily Bread," which is simply a bit of Godly encouragement and wisdom for all I have come to know and love. This went on for a little over a year and finally one Sunday—he came. The seed was planted! He got water every time he came to service, and God gave the increase. In 2008, this same big-time club promoter on his wedding day got baptized in Jesus' name along with his soon to be wife and children. God's glory was displayed further when this same big-time club promoter got filled with the Holy Ghost almost two years later during a Monday night prayer. It excites me to testify that this same big-time club promoter now teaches Sunday school at my church! To this day this young man won't step foot in a club. Not even if I'm doing a gig—it's like pulling teeth to get him there. God is good and he is faithful.

"He that winneth souls is wise." (Proverbs 11:30)

Many people may not step foot in a church, and some may not pick up a Bible. As Christians, our lives are on display, and it's our duty to walk, talk, and live lives that reflect Christ. It's my desire that we hear the heart of God. I challenge you! After each devotional—read, pray, and seek God by digging into His Word. I believe the saint *will* be encouraged, the backslider *will* be restored and renewed, and the sinner *will* be lead to Christ Jesus. Enjoy and be blessed!

"Ye are our epistle written in our hearts, known and read of all men." (II Corinthians 3:2)

Contents

No More Excuses

The question was asked during a church service I was in at the House of Prayer Reformation Church: "What's hindering you?" The conclusion of the matter: "No more excuses."

I can hear "Sweet Brown" saying, "Ain't nobody got time for that!"

God said in his Word, "Knowing the time, that now it is high time to awake out of sleep" (Romans 13:11a).

It's time to get up! Sin has knocked us down, Satan has dropped us, and our own stupid mistakes got us in a daze, but God said, "Wake up!" "Now is our salvation nearer than when we believed. The night is far spent, the day is at hand: let us therefore cast off the works of darkness, and let us put on the armour of light. Let us walk honestly, as in the day; not in rioting and drunkenness, not in chambering and wantonness, not in strife and envying. But put ye on the Lord Jesus Christ, and make not provision for the flesh, to fulfil the lusts thereof" (Romans 13:11–14).

No more excuses; time is now to be saved. Now is the time to repent, forgive, ask for forgiveness, and remove bitterness and strife! We don't have time for all that! It's time to be blessed abundantly.

Love,

JTJR

I'm Straight!

"Prepare ye the way of the Lord, make his paths straight." (Luke 3:4b–6)

Make room for the Lord. Make time for the Lord. Do what needs to be done because he is coming.

"Every valley shall be filled, and every mountain and hill shall be brought low; and the crooked shall be made straight, and the rough ways shall be made smooth; And all flesh shall see the salvation of God." (Luke 3:5–6)

The confusion, depression, and anxiety—the low places many face God shall fill! Everything that seems impossible, every high thing shall be brought down! Everything that's crooked God shall make straight. Things that seem rough—when we yoke up with Christ Jesus, he shall make our burdens light and our yokes easy. Prepare the way. Decrease so that God can increase. Lay aside every weight and sin that easily besets you, delight in the Lord, and see the salvation of the Lord. Understand God is in control, and no matter what's going on in our lives, God is going to make everything straight!

Love,

JTJR

Change My Language

God has given us power and dominion over all that's in the earth. We can train dogs to sit, roll over, and play dead. We have some who can tame lions and wrestle with alligators. SeaWorld has Flipper and killer whales jumping out the water doing back flips. But how can we tame all these animals but can't control our mouths?

> *"For every kind of beasts, and of birds, and of serpents, and of things in the sea, is tamed, and hath been tamed of mankind: But the tongue can no man tame; it is an unruly evil, full of deadly poison." (James 3:7–9)*

Man our mouths will get us in trouble. Selling wolf tickets and bouncing checks our mouths can't cash. Because of lies and rumors, half-truths, many lives have been destroyed. Some have lost jobs, friendships, relationships, and have even been locked up because of lies! Some are in the grave now because of lies. That's why God said all liars shall take their part in the lake of fire.

> *"Out of the same mouth proceedeth blessing and cursing. My brethren, these things ought not so to be." (James 3:10)*

Christians who cuss.... Huh? Don't get the "saint" mad or cut them off while driving; they will cuss you out, and then some like to bring Apostle Peter in to justify their foul language. When all hell broke loose and while Peter was under pressure he started cussing and denying that he ever knew Jesus. But thank God for Jesus because he blessed Peter and knew Peter was "turnt up" before the foundations of the world. But God had a plan for Peter and he was going to use that same tongue to preach the Gospel of Jesus Christ! Some like Peter can't tame the cussing demon. We can't tame our own tongues, but there's one with all power who can. It was on the Day of Pentecost when Peter's language changed! God filled him with the Holy Ghost and he spoke with other tongues, and the people heard him speak of the wonderful works of God!

Let God control your tongue and speak great things and wonderful works of our Lord and Savior Jesus Christ! Lord, change my language.

Love,

JTJR

Born This Way;
Born Again This Way!

Because of sin we are shaped in iniquity and born into a world of sin. When I hear some homosexuals say they were "born 'this way,'" it could be debatable, but there are some who were born with an unnatural condition. In John 9:2–4, Jesus' disciples asked, "Master, who did sin, this man, or his parents, that he was born blind?" Those who are Bible believers and students of the Word know those who were sick and plagued with a disease were linked to some type of sin or a generational curse. Sometimes we get like the disciples when trouble and hell break loose. We try to figure out what we did that was wrong or who in the family is carrying a curse.

But look what Jesus says: "Jesus answered, neither hath this man sinned, nor his parents: but that the works of God should be made manifest in him" (John 9:3).

This man was born blind, and sin wasn't linked to this defect! Some maybe going through and trying to figure out what you did wrong; God said the works of God shall be made manifest!

In verse 6–7 Jesus looked at this young man's issue, spit on the ground, made clay of the spittle, and anointed the blind man with the clay. Jesus told him to wash in the pool of Siloam (which is by interpretation, Sent). Therefore he went his way, washed, and came seeing.

All of us were just like the blind man, in darkness and lost in sin, but then came Jesus! When Jesus expressed his love for me, he gave me instructions on salvation, healing, deliverance, and a better life. Jesus said you must be born again of the water and of the Spirit in Jesus' name. Just like the blind man, I followed God's instructions, and as I repented of my sins, washed in the pool, I came up seeing! Old things were passed away, and behold, all things became new! Those that feel like they were born "this way," be born again! No sin, no sickness, no generational curse will keep you bound; Jesus came to set you free today! If you haven't repented of your sins do it! If you haven't been baptized in water in JESUS' NAME do it! And to the backslider Jesus said, "I'm married to you." Come back home to Jesus, for deliverance, healing, and a better life is for you!

Love,

JTJR

My Desire

"Brethren, my heart's desire and prayer to God for Israel is, that they might be saved." *(Romans 10:1–2)*

Jesus came to save the lost. It's his desire to see us saved. Jesus gave his life for us, and he said it's not his will for any to perish. Those that truly follow Christ and love God—we must have the same love, passion, and compassion. The reality is that the wages of sin is death, but the gift of God is eternal through our Lord and Savior Jesus Christ!

It's my desire for all to know Jesus Christ. Satan has darkened so many minds and hearts and has given the wrong perception of Jesus. But it's my desire for all to know God in a better way! Try him and trust him; your eyes will be open, your life will be changed for the better, and the love of God will overtake you! This is my desire and prayer for all!

Love,

JTJR

Stop Playing House!

Jesus was having a conversation with a woman, and he said in John 4:16–18, "Go, call thy husband, and come hither." The lady replied that she had no husband. "Jesus said unto her, Thou hast well said, I have no husband: (You're right) for thou hast had five husbands; and he whom thou now hast is not thy husband: in that saidst thou truly."

Ladies and gents, this lady was playing house, and the reason why some women can't get a good man or keep one is because they are still playing house. Some are still married to the previous relationship, sex buddy, and one night stand. Here are two reasons why Jesus doesn't want us to fornicate: (1) it's a sin, and (2) when you have sex, the two become one flesh and the soul tie is created. This woman had five husbands and the one she was with wasn't her hubby.

Those that have had multiple partners play the comparison game. Some like them this way and that way, but all you're doing is playing yourself and causing more confusion. It's time to stop playing house. It's time to be healed, saved, and delivered, and break the cycle so we can get who God has for us! No more flesh-mates. God has a soul-mate for you!

Let's renew and refresh our relationship with God. Allow the anointing of God to destroy the ungodly soul ties and yokes so that you can be free! Examine yourself and see if you're still playing house.

Love,

√T√R

I Belong To God

"Let not sin therefore reign in your mortal body, that ye should obey it in the lusts thereof. Neither yield ye your members as instruments of unrighteousness unto sin" (Romans 6:12–13)

Sin is pleasurable. Sin will cause you to compromise your morals and values. Sin will keep you longer than you want to stay, and sin will cost you more than you want to pay. God said don't let sin reign in your body. Don't yield your members as instruments unto sin and unrighteousness. Our bodies don't need to be filled with drank, weed, cocaine, codeine, cigs, curse words, lust, perversion, SIN! The wages of sin is still death. God wants us to "yield yourselves unto God, as those that are alive from the dead, and your members as instruments of righteousness unto God." God wants to use us for his glory. God wants us to do greater works! We must be that royal priesthood and holy nation! Let's yield to God and his righteousness and be a blessing in Jesus' name, amen. We belong to God!

Love,

JTJR

Shake It Off

The enemy comes to kill, steal and destroy. I expect the enemy to do his job especially when I'm on mine.

Apostle Paul was shipwrecked. He got to land, minding his own business gathering sticks, and as he laid the sticks on the fire, "there came a viper out of the heat, and fastened on his hand. And when the barbarians saw the venomous beast hang on his hand, they said among themselves, No doubt this man is a murderer, whom, though he hath escaped the sea, yet vengeance suffereth not to live" (Acts 28:3–5).

When you are living for Christ, haters of Christ will come out of nowhere to take you out. When trouble hits, they will taunt you and ask you where your God is. When you cry loud, spare not, and speak thus, saith the Lord, that demon will lash out. They said no doubt this man is a murderer. Make it personal: no doubt this guy's a fornicator, a dope head, a drunk, a sinner talking that Jesus stuff; he thought he was getting away with something. But I hear God saying from Romans, "who shall lay a charge on Gods elect, it is God who justifies." Don't you worry when men persecute you for the name of Jesus. They can say and do whatever they want but saints of God, those who are living the standard of holiness, verse 5 is for you!

"And he shook off the beast into the fire, and felt no harm."

Don't you trip; just shake the devil off. Poison like doubt, fear, rejection, depression, low self-esteem, alcohol, weed, cigs, perversion, and sin itself tried to penetrate our hearts, but when God is our rock, when we have our Helmet of Salvation, Breastplate of Righteousness, Shield of Faith, waste girted with truth, feet shod with the preparation of the Gospel of Peace, the enemy can neither see us nor stand us. We need to place that devil under our feet and stomp on his head! Be encouraged, saints of God; continue to do the work of the Lord and shake the devil off, and remember: No weapon formed against you shall prosper! Be blessed in Jesus' name.

JTJR

Don't Hang Yourself

"Then Judas, which had betrayed him (Jesus) when he saw that he was condemned, repented himself, and brought again the thirty pieces of silver to the chief priests and elders, saying, I have sinned in that I have betrayed the innocent blood. And they said, What is that to us? see thou to that. And he cast down the pieces of silver in the temple, and departed, and went and hanged himself." (Matthew 27:3–5)

Most of us that love God have a God conscious. The condemnation and conviction kicks in when we sin. But thank God for grace, mercy, and a chance to repent. Judas repented of his sins; he confessed that Jesus was innocent. He tried to return the 30 piece back to the religious people, but they told Judas to keep the money. They got what they wanted, and Judas went and hung himself.

To all backsliders, to those struggling with weights and sins, do what Judas should have done: repent to God and confess your sins to him, for God is faithful and just, to cleanse us from all unrighteousness! Go to Godly council; have them pray and help you through your trying times! Don't stay in your sins, don't beat yourself up, and don't hang yourself. Jesus said in

Isaiah 1:18, *"Come now, and let us reason together, saith the Lord: though your sins be as scarlet, they shall be as white as snow; though they be red like crimson, they shall be as wool."*

Come to Jesus right now; he will save you and deliver you.

Love,

JTJR

Innocent Blood

Innocent blood is being shed all over the world. It's heart breaking to see the violence in Chicago, Illinois. Every day of our lives we must remember the innocent blood which was slain!

"Pilate said unto them, Whom will ye that I release unto you? Barabbas, or Jesus which is called Christ?" (Matthew 27:17–23)

This same question is being asked today! Jesus who works miracles, Jesus who gives us life, or Barabbas, a murderer, a rapist, a liar, a known sinner? The world said Barabbas. "The chief priests and elders persuaded the multitude that they should ask Barabbas, and destroy Jesus."

Pilate asked them again. "They all say unto him, let him be crucified. And the governor said, Why, what evil hath he done? But they cried out the more, saying, Let him be crucified."

Christians are being attacked over this Sodomite agenda. Christians are accused of being haters but Christians, the true saints of God, are praying, loving, and trying to do what is right and pleasing to

God, yet we are being attacked. We must remember the world isn't after us but the Christ in us. Take your cross; stand till the end! Romans 8:36 gave us a fair warning that "we are killed all the day long; we are accounted as sheep for the slaughter." But, Children of the Most High God Jesus Christ, not death, life, angels, principalities, powers, the present time, the future, height, depth, nor any other creature shall separate us from the love of God! Our reward is Heaven! Be encouraged!

Love,

JTJR

GO AND BE A WITNESS

When Jesus got up from the grave, he sent word for his disciples to meet him in Galilee. There Jesus had instructions from Matthew Chapter 28, Mark 16, and Luke 24:47–48. Jesus told them and us to preach and teach the Gospel of Jesus Christ. "Repentance and remission of sins should be preached in his name among all nations, beginning at Jerusalem. And ye are witnesses of these things."

Those that truly love God—we are to be true Jehovah witnesses. To make it clear that Jesus is more than just the Son; he is God Almighty. We are to preach the Gospel of Jesus Christ. Jesus gave us instructions to preach and teach repentance. True repentance is confessing your sins to God and turning your back on sin to live a Godly life. Many have the world's ideology and concept on sin and how to live this life. But we must identify sin and we must share what Jesus did on Calvary for our sins. Once we do that we can tell them that Jesus can put our sins into remission.

Saints of God, today and forever till Jesus comes back, we must spread and share the Gospel. It's time to do our part! Jesus saves!

Love,

JTVR

GET THE FULL PLAN

Most of us have cell phones; there are different plans you can choose from, but there's a plan that offers unlimited everything. Jesus wants us to have the full plan, unlimited everything: salvation!

In some churches it's popular to do a "sinner's prayer" which is nowhere to be found in scripture. Many quote Romans 10:9 and that's it. But we must get back to the teaching of Jesus Christ and all of the scriptures. Before and after the cross, Jesus always preached baptism in water and in the Spirit, in Jesus' name. Jesus told us in John 3:5, "you must be born again of the water and of the Spirit." Jesus said that you cannot enter the Kingdom of God until you do so.

"He that believeth and is baptized shall be saved; but he that believeth not shall be damned" (Mark 16:16).

There's nothing wrong with Romans 10:9, Matthew 28, or Acts 2:38, but we must apply all of the Word. If your local church, pastor, bishop, apostle, whoever he or she is, isn't preaching and teaching all of the Word get out of that place and get the plan of salvation where God's Word is preached in fullness.

"It is written, Man shall not live by bread alone, but by every word that proceedeth out of the Mouth of God" (Matthew 4:4).

Love,

JTJR

Go Forth!

"And they went forth, and preached everywhere, the Lord working with them, and confirming the word with signs following. Amen." (Mark 16:20)

God has given us the power, the authority, and the anointing to win souls! We have the tools! It's time for us to go forth in God. Step out on faith and do the will of God. God is working with us and through us. Miracles, signs, and wonders will follow! Let's get it in and do it big for Jesus!

Love,

JTJR

I Didn't Break Up With You

We are in the last seconds till Jesus returns. Many are falling away from the truth and the Gospel of Jesus Christ. Some are losing their faith. But God said in Isaiah 50:1,

> "Thus saith the Lord, Where is the bill of your mother's divorcement, whom I have put away? or which of my creditors is it to whom I have sold you? Behold, for your iniquities have ye sold yourselves, and for your transgressions is your mother put away."

Jesus said, "I'll never leave you nor forsake you." God has divorced none of his children. He still loves us, still cares for us, and still looks out for us, even when we out of his will! Jesus said, "I'm married to the backslider." The reason there's distance for most is because of sin! "Doing you" is getting *you* in trouble! Living outside the will of God will have your life empty and out of place. If you feel empty, allow God to fill the voids. Jesus said come unto me. Come and let us reason together. It's God who will cleanse us, forgive us and help us. The best place to start is to repent from your sins, receive God's love and allow him to take control. Drugs, alcohol, and lust can't fill the empty places. They can't mend the hurt, but God can. Let him bless you today. Revive your relationship with Jesus today!

Love,

JTJR

Love

"But the fruit of the Spirit is love…" (Galatians 5:22)

Jesus said, "By this shall all men (Mankind) know that ye are my disciples, if you have Love one to another" (John 13:35).

Those who are saved and sanctified, it's our job and our duty to demonstrate and live in love. The Gospel of Jesus Christ, the death, the burial, and the resurrection of our Lord and Savior Jesus Christ are all about love. When you are filled with the Holy Ghost, you are filled with love in its pure form. It's called agape love. This love will rebuke and correct. This love will fight for you and protect you. There's no fear in love. Perfect love casts away all fear. Love saves; love heals; love speaks up; love is God himself, Jesus Christ our Lord!

It's all about love! Do you have love in a hateful and perverse world? Check your fruit, make sure you have love, and live in it!

Love,

JTVR

Joy

"But the fruit of the Spirit is love, joy..."
(Galatians 5:22)

Maybe it's me—I don't know—but on social media I see so many Christians happy one day then mad, cussing, and going off on everybody the next day. Truth be told, some are under demonic oppression, depression, stress and anxiety, which have taken over. Some are even taking pills or drinking just to go to sleep at night! The devil is a lie! If we're truly saved and filled with the Holy Ghost, we must understand that nobody, no demon, is greater than love or joy! Yes, tests and trials come to us all, but God said, "Count it all Joy when you fall into divers temptation." God said, "We glory in tribulation. We glory because we know *all things work together* for the good of them who love God." God is working things out and this is why we must activate joy in the midst of storms! God said, "The joy of the Lord is your strength." If you don't have any joy God said, "Leap for it! Jump for joy, sing for joy, dance for joy! Praise and worship is way better then pills and alcohol!" When you praise God and when you bless him God immediately shows up because he lives in the midst of praise. We can pray and ask God to deliver; we can praise God and invite him in our situation. God is undefeated and full of victory! We have the victory in Jesus! Those that have been feeling low or a lack of joy, open your mouth and begin to give God praise; run, dance, leap, and watch love and joy (God) show up, today and forever more. Live in joy.

Love,

JTJR

Peace

"But the fruit of the Spirit is love, joy, peace..."
(Galatians 5:22)

Our world is out of control and there's no way we can blame God when he gave us dominion and power. Because some don't want to take heed to God's word, they obey the voices of demons. The spirit of murder, hate and rebellion is running wild. Many are seeking peace but seeking it through alcohol, cigs and weed to "calm" their nerves and to get some rest. Some go shopping as therapy but still are not satisfied. Some like myself will take a ride to get away from the noise. I'll hit the beach and that's cool, but before I get there I'm already talking to the Prince of Peace! There is a peace that surpasses all understanding.

Before God left his fleshly body he made a promise to leave his Spirit with us! Thank God for the Holy Spirit. Jesus also said in John 14:27, "Peace I leave with you, my peace I give unto you: not as the world giveth, give I unto you. Let not your heart be troubled, neither let it be afraid."

No need to be afraid, no need to be running wild when you have the Holy Ghost down on the inside! Nothing is greater than love, joy, and peace! God said,

"I'll keep him/her in perfect peace whose mind is stayed on thee." There's nothing like a peace of mind. Get your mind on Jesus, live in the Spirit of God and may the rest of your days be in love, joy, and peace.

Love,

JTJR

SPEAK FOR YOURSELF; I AM PERFECT!

There's a fallacy that has been taught as truth. We have been taught that "nobody is perfect." But according to the Word of God that's a lie. Now I know the intent in which many are saying that but God's Word is absolute truth. Look what God says in Job 1:1:

> *"There was a man in the land of Uz, whose name was Job; and that man was perfect and upright, and one that feared God, and eschewed evil."*

Here's a man who was perfect. Perfect doesn't mean he didn't go through anything. Perfect doesn't mean he walked on water. Apostle Peter walked on water and we all know he was far from perfect. Ha, ha. So walking on water isn't a requirement in being perfect. Perfect means he obeyed Gods Word and lived according to God's Spirit, and we all know God Almighty is *perfect*!

Yes, we all have sinned, but we don't have to live in sin. We all have some type of issue or a thorn that keeps us humble, but know God's grace is sufficient for you! We must eliminate every excuse that the world, the devil and what we come up with! Take the limits off God! Jesus said in Matthew 5:48, "Be ye therefore perfect, even as your Father which is in heaven is perfect." When somebody says you're not perfect, tell them to speak for themselves, God says something else about me! Be what God commanded you to be, be holy, be righteous, and be perfect!

Have a perfect day in Jesus!

Love,

JTVR

KINGDOM LIVING

"And he said unto them, Take heed, and beware of covetousness: for a man's life consisteth not in the abundance of the things which he possesseth." (Luke 12:15)

Many people have the wrong perspective on life. Many are on the paper chase and for other material possessions. Nothing wrong with material possessions, but that's not life itself! What profit any to gain the whole world but lose their soul? Life is nothing but a vapor.

Children of the Most High God Jesus Christ, we are to have a Kingdom-minded state and Kingdom perspective on life. The Kingdom of God is joy, peace, love, and righteousness in the Holy Ghost. Jesus said, "Seek ye first the kingdom of God and his righteousness and all these things shall be added unto you." No need to trip or stress. Jesus said, "Fear not, little flock; for it is your Father's good pleasure to give you the kingdom." God wants us to have abundant life. But we must have a desire for God! Don't get caught up in things. Don't get caught up chasing blessings; chase after God, bless him and let the blessings chase you.

Kingdom-minded people have their eyes set on Heaven. We must continue in Holy Living. We must pray, fast, seek God's Word daily because we don't know when God will take us home. Today and forever let's have a mind to serve the Lord.

Love,

JTJR

I KNOW I'M FAVORED

Every day and every Sunday my father/pastor gets up and speaks life to us. He gets up and says, "Has anyone told you today that you're loved and highly favored … if not I'll be the first to tell you that you are loved and highly favored."

Sometimes it's hard to believe because at times we aren't so loveable. Sometimes we don't feel favored because life's situations don't look or feel too good. But we have to go back to children's church and say, "Yes, Jesus loves me; this I know, for the Bible tells me so." You better believe and know God's Word! Jesus said in his Word concerning us, "while we were yet sinners Christ Died." That's love for all!

Every day Satan goes to God and accuses us of all kinds of stuff. And of most stuff we are guilty and worthy of death! But God, who is rich in mercy, gives us a chance to repent! When we truly repent, God washes our sins away and forgets them! After the accuser tells all, Jesus sees nothing but the blood! You better believe God loves and favors you! You know you've messed up and done wrong. We're not getting away with anything, but God is still blessing us! Even when we are living holy and upright, a storm can arise and it tries to consume us, but God's love and favor will arise.

God's love and favor will protect us from all hurt, harm and danger! When foul spirits come at us, Jesus knows how to lift up a standard against the enemy!

VICTORY!

"By this I know that thou favourest me, be-cause mine enemy doth not triumph over me."
(Psalms 41:11)

The world is losing every battle because it doesn't have God's favor! But those who are in Christ Jesus haven't lost a battle yet! There's no losing in love or favor in Christ Jesus. If you feel like you're losing or getting the short end of the stick, examine your relationship with Christ. Are you seeking God? Are you being faithful over a few things? Are you being a witness and living by the greatest commandment, which is love? If you don't know Jesus or need refreshing, today is your day for a fresh start and to live in love and favor with God! Victory is yours today! Know that you are loved and highly favored by God!

Love,

JTJR

I'M NOT MOVED!

Saved and unsaved in our country, the United States, we all have experienced what third-world countries experience on a regular basis. Unexpected explosions and tragedies are taking a toll on us in America. It's sad because right here in our country gang violence, murders, kidnappings rape, etc., is happening every day. We all wonder why at times, but we must remember that Satan comes to kill, steal, and destroy. But God's Word always brings us encouragement in tough times.

God said in 2 Thessalonians 2:2, "Be not soon shaken in mind, or be troubled, neither by spirit, nor by word, nor by letter as from us, as that the day of Christ is at hand."

Don't be shaken! Guard your minds with the Helmet of Salvation! Our spirits may be troubled but Jesus said in John Chapter 14, "Let not your Heart be troubled"! Please understand, God is in control and he won't let this fire get out of hand! Satan can't have his way fully. No matter what the world says, no matter what the Congress or the President says, Jesus Christ God Almighty is King! Keep standing, keep praying, believing and receiving God's Word! We shall survive, we shall live and we will live life more abundantly! Don't you give up on God; he's not through blessing you. Put all your faith and trust in Jesus, and he will see you through! Let us pray for this nation and our world that we repent and turn to God so healing can take place in Jesus' name!

Love,

JTJR

I'm Good!

"I'm good" is a phrase that is used in many ways. When somebody gets mad or upset and they try to play cool or downplay the situation they say, "I'm good." If anybody is like me, when it comes to snacks y'all will say, "I'm good." Ha, ha. Yes, Lord. No matter what is going on in our lives Jesus wants us to be good! Our character, our integrity, and our attitude must be good! We must take a page from Joseph. Joseph was favored by God and his parents. His brothers hated on him and they even sold him into slavery. But God favored Joseph even while he was a slave. You could be placed in a bad situation, but know God will be right there with you!

Genesis 39:2–6 says the Lord was with Joseph and everything he put his hands to prospered! No matter what you're going through, child of God, he will prosper you! Joseph found grace in the sight of his master and he served him: and he made him overseer over his house, and all that he had he put into his hand. You better believe the blessings of the Lord is on you!

"And it came to pass from the time that they had made him overseer in his house, and over all that he had, that The Lord blessed the Egyptian's

house for Joseph's sake; and the blessing of the Lord was upon all that he had in the house, and in the field. And Joseph was a goodly person and well favoured."

What the devil meant for evil, God is turning it around for your good. All things work together for our good. The blessings of Joseph—he maintained his faith, and he remembered God's promises and Word. He lived with character and integrity, and that's what made him a Godly person. We ought to do the same! Stay classy, don't compromise and be ratched! Stand for God's righteousness and allow the favor of the Lord to overtake you! Please believe, when you do this, you will say, "I'm good."

Love,

JTJR

DELIVERANCE IN A DIRTY SITUATION

Saints of God, we are in the world, not of the world, but we also know evil communications corrupt good manners! Every day we have to fight our flesh just to maintain and obtain salvation! Many of us need deliverance. In 2 Kings 5:1–14, there was a man named Naaman who was a mighty man in valor, but he was a leper. Yes, some of us are spotty and have a past, but don't let your past dictate your future! There's deliverance from your spots!

Even being sick, Naaman remained faithful to God! So God sent a Word of deliverance and healing for him. Please believe this Word today is a Word of deliverance for you in Jesus' name! Naaman went to the city to see the Prophet Elisha but Elisha sent a messenger saying, "Go and wash in Jordan seven times, and thy flesh shall come again to thee, and thou shalt be clean."

But most church goers, like Naaman, hear the Word but complain, give their opinion and don't receive the Word. Naaman, like most that have issues, wanted the Man of God to call his name, lay hands and open up the windows of Heaven. But the Man of God told him to go in a dirty and nasty river to be cleaned from his sickness! God will ask us to do some crazy stuff at times but please believe glory will come out of it!

Naaman's servant came near, and said, "if the prophet had bid thee do some great thing, wouldst thou not have done it? How much rather then, when he saith to thee, Wash, and be clean?"

Thank God for friends that will talk sense into us. Naaman came to his senses and "dipped himself seven times in Jordan, according to the saying of the man of God: and his flesh came again like unto the flesh of a little child, and he was clean."

Stop doing you, stop doing what you think or seems right and obey God's Word which is absolutely right! Your healing and your deliverance depends on it! I encourage all to do God's will and be saved, delivered, and set free from a dirty, unhealthy situation! Today is your day!

Love,

JTJR

Don't Make It Hard On Yourself!

Many say life is hard. Many say living for God is hard. But the truth is, we make it hard at times. God said in Proverbs 13:15b, "The way of transgressors is hard."

Sin will have you living a hard life. Sin will add years on your life. Some are 30 years old but looking 60 years old? Why live the hard-knock life when you can live the good life in Christ Jesus?

In this life, saved and unsaved people will have ups and downs, but why make things worse with weed and other drugs when you can call on Jesus and he will bring you peace?! Why be a hoe and sleep around for money and pleasure when God will supply all you need according to his riches in glory? Why be bound to depression, stress, fear, and un-forgiveness when Jesus said, "Take my yoke for my yoke is easy and my burden is light"? Stop making things hard in your life and live for Jesus. He is the author and finisher of our faith!

Peace,

JTJR

Sounds Good But I Need More Than That!

A man said, "I'll give you the sun, the moon, and the stars." He said he would buy food, clothes, and pay rent for his girl.

First of all, you're crazy, sir. Ha, ha. All that for a woman you're not married to? And, Bruh, don't lie; you can't give what doesn't belong to you. The moon, the stars, etc., belong to God! Vain and enticing words don't get you anything but disappointments! This is why Jesus said, "Let every man be a lie but my Word True."

Apostle Paul said in 1 Corinthians 2:4–5, 13, "And my speech and my preaching was not with enticing words of man's wisdom, but in demonstration of the Spirit and of power."

Whenever a man or a woman of God speaks, teaches, counsels, or preaches under the anointing and speaks thus saith the Lord, things will happen! They're not speaking from man's wisdom, nor do they speak what they think, but they speak from the oracles of God and when God speaks it comes to pass!

Friends and family, "your faith should not stand on the wisdom of men, but in the power of God."

We have plenty of doctors on TV and counselors using man's wisdom and enticing words but they can't fix anyone's life until they yield to the voice of God and speak thus saith the Lord. This is why Jesus said, "Blessed is the man that walketh not in the Counsel of the ungodly." Jesus is our counselor. Jesus will send men and women of God to counsel, and he speaks truth and words of life unto us. Jesus will send us pastors after his own heart!

Talk is cheap and many of us are tired of the games, gimmicks, and manipulation. It's time for manifestation! Seek God and allow him to direct your path; see and experience the power and demonstration of his Spirit! Miracles and blessings will take place!

Love,

√TJR

I'm Not Ashamed!

I must be transparent. I grew up in a sanctified house, where the Lord rested, ruled and abided, where Godly principles, morals and values were taught. As a teen, trying to be "grown," I hid condoms in my closet just in case they needed to be used. The cold part is I was too scared to do anything, let alone in my house because the Lord was there. As we come to understand, the Lord is everywhere, beholding the good and the evil! But I had respect for my parents and their house, and I knew things like that in the house were wrong, so I had to hide them!

The reason why killers, rapists, liars, homosexuals and others who are involved with different type of sins keep secrets and hide in the closet is because they know it's wrong! All of us have a God conscious even if we reject it. Now, if we reject it enough, God will turn us over to a reprobate mind, and we don't want to get to that place.

We must understand that sin will never be accepted in God's eyes, but Satan has made sin popular. It's popular to be the "Baddest B," to get that "loud" weed and blow it in the air, pop Molly's and sweat. It's popular to be gangsta. Sin is glorified in our world and it's acceptable to some without shame! Some even promote that they are "shameless." People see no wrong nor do they see the big deal! But on the contrary, it's a big deal because the wages of sin is still death! But there's a better way to live, and I'm not ashamed to tell it!

> *"For I am not ashamed of the gospel of Christ: for it is the power of God unto salvation to every one that believeth" (Romans 1:16).*

I'm not ashamed to say I've repented of my sins. I'm baptized in Jesus' name and filled with the Holy Ghost. I speak in tongues, and I run, dance, leap, and shout for joy! I'm not ashamed to tell the goodness of Jesus! I'm not ashamed to stand for God! I'm not ashamed to say I live by faith. I'm living life more abundantly and there's no way I can make it without the Lord! I'm glad I'm saved and I know I'm saved! Saints of God, it's time to come out of the closet and lift up the name of Jesus!

Love,

JTJR

Your Love Saved My Life

Loving parents' and grandparents' houses are baby-proofed till the baby or babies get to a certain age. I don't know what it is, but babies like to stick their hands on or in wall sockets. If a child is trying to play with the sockets, their parents and grandparents will cry out, "No! Stop!" Some babies will proceed anyways, and most of the time they get their hand slapped. The baby may cry but it will understand later that mom and dad were keeping them from hurting and killing themselves.

Jesus is our Heavenly Father, and yes, he loves us!

> *"For whom the Lord loveth he chasteneth, and scourgeth every son whom he receiveth."* *(Hebrews 12:6–8)*

Yup, we are God's babies, and yes, we get into stuff we have no business being in! God tells us, "No" and "Stop," but sometimes we proceed to do what we want. God will correct us and break out that strap if needed because he loves us! Yup, we may cry but then we will be just like King David and say, "It was good for me that I've been afflicted. I'd rather get this whooping so my life will be saved!" Thank you,

Lord, for loving us enough not to allow us to live in error! We ought to thank God for the times he told us no and sent us warning. Please understand that God loves us and has our best interests at heart.

Love,

JTJR

Come Correct

Have you've ever met somebody that will call you and just start talking, or just start complaining, or start asking for favors without asking how you're doing? Man, it makes me shake my head. Sometimes when I run into people like that, before I allow the conversation to continue, I respond by saying, "I'm doing fine, thanks for asking. And how are you?"

Quiet as it's kept, some of us come at God the same way. We have to do better and come correct. We need to have some respect and reverence for the Lord of lords and King of kings.

The disciples pleaded with Jesus, "Teach us how to pray."

Some of us don't know how to pray, and sometimes we don't even know what to say or pray for, but thank God for the Holy Ghost who intercedes for us. We must get in the Spirit when we pray.

Psalms 100:4 encourages us to "Enter into his gates with thanksgiving".

Every day we ought to give thanks! When we come to God, let's enter with thanksgiving.

Let's enter "into his courts with praise". There's much we can complain about. There's so much we can cry about, but complaining and crying won't fix our situations; however, praise will! For the Lord dwells in the midst of praise. If the Lord doesn't bring you out, invite him in and let him change the situation for the better.

"… be thankful unto him, and bless his name."

Praise him for who he is and thank him for what he has done. Praise and thanks must be continual! While you bless the name of Jesus, God is blessing you. When we get into praise and thanks, we will find ourselves in worship mode. God will open our eyes and we will see how blessed we really are when we enter and come correctly. We will see all the ways he has made for us. We will see the miracles that took place in our lives; the complaints and tears will cease, and joy will overtake us.

From now on, let's come correct. When we wake up, let's thank the Lord! When we find ourselves in horrible situations, thank God for being a deliverer! Before we step foot into church, have praise in your heart, mind, body, soul, and spirit, and open your mouth to magnify him! Let everything that has breath praise Ye, the Lord!

Let's come correct.

Love,

JTJR

Behave Yourself!

"And David behaved himself wisely in all his ways; and the Lord was with him." (1 Samuel 18:14)

I see so many people posting so many videos on social media of people just wild 'n out. People post long messages to their "haters," cussing and saying they're praying for the person, but they just look foolish and ignorant while the devil sits back and laughs. We must understand that Satan comes to kill, steal, and destroy. He will try anything and do anything to provoke us to sin and turn our backs on God. Somebody could be acting ugly, cussing you out, and threatening you; Satan is waiting for you to react ungodly, but we must behave ourselves in all our ways and use wisdom! God said, "Be angry but sin not." Don't even let "the sun go down on your wrath."

Don't you know God can handle your situations better then you? Don't entertain the devil.

"Neither give place to the devil." (Ephesians 4:27)

Behave yourself! Satan will tempt us with things we like, for sin is pleasurable. The ungodly and those you sin with will remind you, saying, "I thought you were saved." Don't forget the wages of sin is death! We all get tempted but we must live in the Spirit, deny our flesh, and behave ourselves wisely! In this text, David was going through it. Saul was jealous of David; he tried to kill David but David behaved himself and the Lord was with him. When God is on your side, there's nothing the devil can do! No weapon formed against the children of God shall prosper.

We all fell for Satan's traps and snares, so let's repent, stay focused, and let's not get beside ourselves and out of character. Let's behave ourselves!

Love,

JTJR

Thank You!

We have to thank God for some demons. There are some demons that will provoke us to do right. We have some that are waiting for us to fall and mess up so they can say, "I thought you were saved, talking this God stuff, but you did this, that and the other." Satan will always remind you of your past but remind him of his future! Your past and what you did yesterday is not in your now! We have new mercies every morning!

But it's a blessing because these types of demons will keep us humble, and it reminds us that we are in this sinful nature, and sinful flesh, we must crucify daily. We must yield to God and live in the spirit, because in the flesh we have the potential to wild out!

Yes, we are saved by grace *but* through faith; we still have to put some work in when it comes to salvation.

We don't just say "I do" and "I will" when we get married and that's it; you must work at the marriage. It's the same with this walk with Christ. We are instructed in Philippians 2:12, "work out your own salvation with fear and trembling."

The lifestyle we live as Christians is still holiness. Strive for holiness daily. If you fall or mess up, don't give up! Get back up and aim for holiness. Don't get caught up in your feelings, because Satan will make you feel like you're not saved and delivered. No, repent and get up. Allow God to deliver you and sanctify you.

Be encouraged, stay focused and live for Jesus!

Love,

JTJR

It's About Time!

"But the end of all things is at hand: be ye there-fore sober, and watch unto prayer." (1 Peter 4:7)

I don't know the trial, the trouble or the storm you may be facing, but God said the end of it *all* is at hand! It's time to sober up and stop tripping. Cast away doubt and fear. Cast away depression and anxiety in the name of Jesus. Watch and pray. Open up your spiritual eyes and pray in the Spirit; call those things that be not as though they are! As you tap into the Spirit in the mist of prayer, give God thanks! While you're in praise mode, you will see yourself past the finish line. It's about time for *victory*! Keep pressing forward, child of God!

Stay and be encouraged!

Love,

JTJR

He's Turning It!

In this life, we will suffer, and we will experience pain. In this walk with Christ, we will experience betrayal and persecution for his name sake. They hated Jesus and they will hate on you. The world will rejoice in your heartache, pain and distress, but in spite of it all Jesus said in John 16:20b, "But your sorrow shall be turned into joy."

All that you've gone through and experienced for the name of Jesus—God is turning it around for your good! Your sorrow is turning into joy, and if you believe God and his Word, it's time to rejoice and receive joy now!

Love,

JTJR

Cheaters, Treat God Better!

"The eyes of the Lord are in every place, beholding the evil and the good." (Proverbs 15:3)

Whether we know it or not, all of us have been on the show *Cheaters*. All of us have declared that we love God, yet we all have flirted with the devil, slept in on Sunday mornings, given glory and credit to our education, gifts and talents. God has been faithful, done miracles, blessed us when we didn't deserve it, loves us unconditionally, yet we cheat on him. Then we have the nerve to say, "God knows my heart." Yes, he knows that the heart is deceitfully wicked. Yes, we make mistakes and we fall, but our God is powerful enough to keep us from falling.

If Jesus is your Lord and Savior and you have a "personal relationship," don't allow your sins to be a crutch! Allow God to be your help and support! We can't live perfectly if we don't allow Christ to rest, rule and abide in us.

In this relationship with God, make sure the relationship isn't one sided! Be faithful, love God, love his people, hate sin, and do his will! Don't worry about the fake ones. They will call you "holier than thou," but take it as a compliment because you under-stand the standard is still holiness. No more excuses. Let's treat God better than before!

Love,

JTVR

Go Out On A Limb

We live in a day where many people take risk. It's risky business sleeping on the job because there's a possibility you'll get caught. Ha, ha. Many people take a risk on investments and different opportunities that can either make or break a person. Taking a risk is a page out of faith. It takes faith to do things that seems impossible. Faith makes the impossible possible!

In Luke 19:2–5, there was a man named Zacchaeus, who had mad pull; he was chief among the publicans, and he was rich. But this man heard about Jesus, and he wanted to see him for himself. The problem was he was short and there were others longing to see Jesus. So instead of fighting through the crowd, "he ran before, and climbed up into a sycamore tree to see him: for he was to pass that way."

We have to learn how to get Ahead of the game. We can't get caught up in the crowd; we have to follow the leading of the Lord and we must do it in a hurry. This man ran and climbed in a tree. Sometimes we have to do what needs to be done to see Jesus! The question must be asked: what's keeping you from seeing Jesus, what's keeping you from receiving the promises of God? It's time to run and chase after God.

> *"And when Jesus came to the place, he looked up, and saw him, and said unto him, Zacchaeus, make haste, and come down; for to day I must abide at thy house."*

I don't know what you need from the Lord, but I dare you to step out on faith and go out on a limb! Today is your day; God is going to abide in you and your house.

Love,

JTJR

He Nailed It

Many people are living in regret, guilt, and shame; their sins are consuming them. But why live like that? Why allow the devil to rule your life? God said in Colossians 2:14,

> *"Blotting out the handwriting of ordinances that was against us, which was contrary to us, and took it out of the way, nailing it to his cross..."*

Let us be grateful for *conviction* of Spirit. Let us also be grateful that we serve a God who is merciful and full of grace. When we repent and confess our sins, Jesus is faithful and just to cleanse us from all unrighteousness. There is no need to live in regret, guilt and shame, when you live after God with a re-pented heart. Every sin that we have carried out was nailed to the cross! Leave your sins on the cross! Lay your burdens on the altar and live life in freedom in Christ Jesus.

Peace,

JTJR

Are You Fit?

Every year at the beginning of the year, many people talk about getting fit for the summer. Ladies got dresses they are trying to get into. Fellas are trying to get swole. Gyms across the land get jam-packed. The sacrifice and the dedication is serious. The pain is real, but the results are rewarding. But the many quickly turn into few and chances are the many aren't fit.

Likewise, we have many who start out the year in church, being faithful to God, but as soon as trouble comes, the pain comes, many leave the church thinking they can do better without God. In truth, they're not fit either.

"Jesus said unto him, No man, having put his hand to the plough, and looking back, is fit for the kingdom of God." (Luke 9:62)

Don't be a quitter, don't be a church drop out; get back on it and get fit. The reward and the results are better with God! Get your membership back with

Christ! With Christ there is a life-time warranty and he paid it all! Membership is free indeed!

Peace,

√T√R

"The Highway, Get On The Freeway"

From California, we will never make it to Florida going north or south. In order for us to get to Florida from Cali, our best bet is to get on Interstate 10 East and take it straight out.

In this life there are many roads, highways and freeways, but if we're not careful will we find ourselves going in circles, running into dead ends and getting lost.

Truth is we all went down the wrong direction and highway. Some of us drove to the liquor store, the smoke shop, the strip club, and the dope man's spot. We've found ourselves driving to the same type of ungodly, unhealthy relationships, going in circles. Then, many got in the fast lane on the express way, some crashed and burned, and some didn't survive. God said in Proverbs 16:17, "The highway of the upright is to depart from evil: he that keepeth his way preserveth his soul."

It's time to get on the right highway because our lives depend on it!

There's only one way to live, only one highway that can take us to where we need to go. The name of the highway is also a freeway; Isaiah 35:8 states, "And an highway shall be there, and a way, and it shall be called The way of holiness; the unclean shall not pass over it; but it shall be for those: the wayfaring men, though fools, shall not err therein."

Jesus is the only way to abundant living. Jesus is the way the truth and the life. It's called a freeway because Jesus paid the cost on Calvary. Holiness is the way to Heaven. I encourage all to get on the Highway of Holiness and coast to a better and everlasting life.

Peace,

JTJR

LIFE SAVERS

I don't know about y'all, but when I was a kid I loved Life Savers. And of course, the red ones were the best ones in my opinion. But the candy is unique; it's shaped like a lifebuoy ring. If a person falls overboard, somebody throws out a lifebuoy to prevent them from drowning. In this life, God has sent us a Life Saver!

"For the Son of man is not come to destroy men's lives, but to save them." (Luke 9:56 KJV)

The devil comes to kill, steal and destroy. He wants us drunk, tipsy and high. He has designed ungodly habits, friendships and relationships that will cause us to go under. He has lied on God and has us believing God is in Heaven sending down lightning bolts and killing folk. The devil is a lie; Jesus came to save us from a burning Hell. He came to keep us from drowning in our sins. And those that are saved he sent out as more Life Savers to save others! Thank God for saved family members, friends and even strangers that became Life Savers. We may not like to hear correction and rebuke, but that love will save our lives. Thank God for Life Savers and thank

God for Jesus who is our Life Savior. We all are in need of Life Savior and we need to be a Life Saver!

Love,

JTJR

JUST LIKE HIM

Everywhere I go people that see me see my father and vice versa. It's tough to avoid it, because I think I'm cute and him ... well ... no comment.

When Jesus was getting ready to be nailed on the cross, Apostle Peter was nearby and the people said, "He was with him; he's one of them." Peter tried to deny it, but no matter what, he couldn't, and we can't deny who we are in Christ Jesus.

We are created in God's image and his likeness. Even though sin enters our flesh, there is God in all of us. We can't allow this deadbeat father named Satan to ruin or run our lives anymore. Sin has separated us, but through Jesus Christ and his blood, it's possible for us to be free from the curse of sin; we can now have fellowship and a relationship with our Heavenly Father. Don't deny Christ. We can't run from him; allow Jesus to be that Great Father in your life. Living a bastard's life is whack. Let's be more like our Heavenly Father. Repent, be baptized in Jesus' name, be filled with God's Spirit. Jesus said in Matthew 5:48, "Be ye therefore perfect, even as your Father which is in heaven is perfect." It's time to be perfect, time to be like Christ.

Love,

JTJR

I'M ON IT

"Take heed now; for the Lord hath chosen thee to build an house for the sanctuary: be strong, and do it." (1 Chronicles 28:10)

Now is the time for the children of God to arise and put in work. Satan is on his job and it's time for us to be on ours. We must build a house, a sanctuary where God can dwell. The foundation must be built on Christ Jesus. In this text, Solomon was called to build God a house, but God is also speaking to us in the spiritual. We must allow God to work in us, through us and live in us. For our bodies are the temple of the Lord. It's time to kick Satan out; he's been a squatter for too long. He's been living rent free, destroying our temple with drugs, alcohol, and ungodliness, putting holes in our hearts and stealing things that don't belong to him. Now is the time to say, "As for me and my house, we shall serve the Lord;" we shall live holy and righteous. We shall uplift and encourage our brothers and sisters in the Lord.

Now is the time and God has given us power and authority. Be strong and do it!

Love,

JTJR

Correct Your Focus

Many of us have the right intentions but the wrong focus. Most of the time we allow the lust of the flesh, lust of the eye, and pride of life to distort our vision. And without a vision, the people perish! In all things we must see how God sees.

> "But the Lord said unto Samuel, Look not on his countenance, or on the height of his stature; because I have refused him: for the Lord seeth not as man seeth; for man looketh on the outward appearance, but the Lord looketh on the heart." (1 Samuel 16:7)

Most of us have made mistakes in relationships because we went outside God's will, got caught up on the outward appearance, and failed to look at the heart. Yes, puppies are cute, but they grow up and reality will kick in: it was a dog the whole time! We make bad investments because things sound good and look good, but we find out as time passes, or sometimes immediately, it's no good!

We truly need to see and know what's really important in life. Our relationship with Christ is more important than anything. Our life on this earth is but a vapor. Here today, gone tomorrow. Our soul must be saved. God must be first! God knows our hearts and desires. He already reigns on the just and unjust, but to get all that he has for us, we must delight ourselves in him.

Make Jesus a part of your plans, partner up with him, follow his vision, and see how God blesses your life greatly because you're walking and living with the correct focus.

Love,

JTJR

Go!

In John Chapter 9:1–7, there was a man who was blind from birth. Jesus spat on the ground, anointed the man's eyes with clay, and told him to go wash in the pool of Siloam. There are things that have happened that we have no control over, yet God will get the glory for in our lives.

Jesus has anointed us, blessed us, and yet we still have issues of dysfunction. We can't allow dysfunction and issues of life to hinder us, because God isn't through with us yet. This man was anointed and blind, but he wasn't deaf. Jesus told him to go to the pool and wash. If you want to be healed and made whole, if you want God to work the impossible, you have to follow God's Word! You have to go to the place of deliverance. Jesus said, "the just shall live by faith". Faith cometh by hearing and hearing the Word of God. This blind man went to the pool of deliverance, and as he washed he was healed and made whole. He was once blind but now can see.

Go to Jesus, follow his instructions, believe by faith and watch God bless you!

Love,

JTJR

IN LOVE WITH A
STRANGE ONE

God has told us all to stay away from the strange things.

But let's be honest: we all fell in love with something strange! Some of us have been in strange relationships. Some of y'all are still in the strange relationship. Some call it complicated. Some are in love with ink, pain and bondage, money, happy-hour alcohol, drugs; the list goes on, it gets stranger, and it's tainting our lives unknowingly like cancer. Sin is a cancer; it starts small and then it grows out of control.

> *"But king Solomon loved many strange women, together with the daughter of Pharaoh, women of the Moabites, Ammonites, Edomites, Zidonians, and Hittites..." (1 Kings 11:1–3)*

Solomon was God's elect and was the wisest man ever; he knew the word, yet he was in love with the enemy of God. His love for strange things became great. He didn't like the church women (which leaves me shaking my head).

The "Lord said unto the children of Israel, Ye shall not go in to them, neither shall they come in unto you: for surely they will turn away your heart after their gods: Solomon clave unto these in love … his wives turned away his heart."

Examine your life. Who has your heart? Who have you linked up with, who are you chillin' with? Are your activities keeping you from being faithful to God? Don't yoke up with anything or anybody that's not connected to God or the blessings of God. If they are not trying to be saved and living holy, then bounce! Smoking and drinking are not of God, so let's do away with that. Our bodies are the temple of the Lord; do away with the tats. Don't get anymore; God doesn't want us to mark our bodies. The things that displease God—let's turn from them and turn back to God and please him.

Peace,

JTJR

THIS IS THE REASON...
KEEP GOING

Many go to church for different reasons. Some go because the music is banging, or they got some fine women or fine brothers in there. Maybe they go because the church is big, the pastor is cool, or the homies go. That's all good and fine, but we have to get to the place where we go because *Jesus is there*. Some friends and family have left. The music department may not crack like it use too. Our worship isn't based on them or that; our worship is based on Jesus Christ and him alone.

Jesus said in Matthew 15:30, 32, "And great multitudes came unto him…"

We need to have a mind to go see the King of kings and Lord of lords. The blessing is we can go to Jesus with our problems and our issues. Jesus came to save the lost.

> "… having with them those that were lame, blind, dumb, maimed, and many others, and cast them down at Jesus' feet; and he healed them …"

I don't know what's wrong with you, I don't know what you're in need of, but lay it all on the altar! Lay it down at the feet of Jesus and allow God to heal you. We're all in need of healing; this is why you ought to be in church on a regular basis. Happy hour, a blunt, a cig, or shopping "therapy" can't fix or solve your problems, but Jesus can! Somebody you know is in need of healing and we ought to intercede for them.

> *"Then Jesus called his disciples unto him, and said, I have compassion on the multitude, because they continue with me …"*

God knows what you're in need of, but can you bless him with your issues, with your sickness? Can you bless him without a job, car, and money? Is your love based on how you feel and what material things you can get, or do you really have a heart and love for God? The Lord is merciful, kind, and compassionate to his people. He wants to bless you and do greater things in your life.

Don't give up. Keep going. Don't let "people" gossip, or derision from the enemy stop you from being in church. In God's presence is where we need to be. If you fell off, get back on; if you feel discouraged, allow the Word to encourage you. Be healed, saved, and set free, and live for Jesus!

Love,

JTJR

I'd Rather Be In The House

There's truly no place like home. My house is filled with love, joy, and peace. It's a refuge, filled with wisdom. It's a blessing and I don't take it for granted, because there are some homes that are filled with dysfunction, cussing, fighting, drugs, alcohol, random women and men, abuse, etc. These things ought not to be, and it's time for house cleaning.

> *"Blessed are they that dwell in thy house: they will be still praising thee. Selah. For a day in thy courts is better than a thousand. I had rather be a doorkeeper in the house of my God, than to dwell in the tents of wickedness." (Psalm 84:4, 10 KJV)*

There's no place like church, the temple in which God dwells. Those who are in the house are blessed. In the house, praise goes up and when praise goes up, Jesus shows up, because he lives in the midst of praise. There's no place like his holy sanctuary. A day being in God's presence is better than anything! I'd rather be an usher in church than be outside in the world of the wicked.

If you don't like your living situation, the power of prayer, praise, and worship will change the atmosphere. The devil will flee, and God will rest, rule, and abide. The church of the Lord Jesus Christ is where every believer should be found. Let's get in and stay in the house.

Peace,

JTJR

Beware Of Perverts

Pervert: Abnormal, distorted, unacceptable corruption, altered from its original course.

Our judicial system is perverted. Our government and Congress are perverted. The entertainment field is perverted. We even have some perverted preachers, leaders, and pastors!

> *"I marvel that ye are so soon removed from him that called you into the grace of Christ unto another gospel: Which is not another; but there be some that trouble you, & would pervert the gospel of Christ." (Galatians 1:6–9)*

Many are troubled, lost, and far-off, because we have too many denominations and too many different beliefs. There's only one gospel, one church, one body, and one God, and his name is *Jesus Christ*. Many are troubled about baptism in Jesus' name. Many are troubled on what day to gather on.

God said through Apostle Paul,

> *"But though we, or an angel from heaven, preach any other gospel unto you than that which we have preached unto you, let him be accursed."*

Jesus told us we must be born again of the water and of the Spirit in his name! Whatsoever we do in word or in deed, do it all in the name of the Lord Jesus Christ. Those that preach against baptism got it wrong according to scripture. Those that don't preach against sin got it wrong according to Holy scriptures. We can't allow perverts to twist the scriptures to get money and rob the people. We can't allow folk to twist the scriptures to justify their sins. It's time for us to be holy. Perverts don't preach teach nor live truth. If your pastor isn't reading and teaching the Word in truth, it's time to go and get in truth. The only way to know truth is to study God's Word.

"As we said before, so say I now again, If any man preach any other gospel unto you than that ye have received, let him be accursed." Get in truth, stay in truth, and get away from the perverts!

Peace,

JTJR

IT'S COMING

"The Lord will give grace & glory: no good thing will he withhold from them that walk uprightly." (Psalm 84:11b)

No matter what we face, no matter what we go through, don't allow your circumstances to consume you. Don't allow ungodliness to keep you from your promises. In fact, keep living for God just because he is God! He has done enough ... please believe the Lord will give grace, favor, and glory to his people. You're going to make it and you will be all right. When you keep God first, when you're faithful in church and in the work of the Lord, when you stand for Jesus and live Godly, God said no good thing will he withhold from you. Keep living upright; your good thing is headed your way!

Love,

JTJR

The God Of A Second Chance

I use to wonder: how can God be the God of a second chance when I blew it more than once? I've sinned more than once.

But I pray you catch this: when we truly repent of our sins, God forgives us. Not only does he forgives, he forgets! And those who claim to be saved need to have God's Spirit which forgives and forgets! Because we all have sinned, we all have done wrong, but God forgives and forgets to the point where he doesn't remember or hold account of all of our sins. That part will take the Holy Ghost with fire to do; Amen, saints.

When we repent and confess our sins, God sends our sins to the place of no remembrance. This is seen in Isaiah 38:17 and Jeremiah 31:34.

Secondly, God sends our sins to the place of no recovery.

"He will turn again, He will have compassion upon us; He will subdue our iniquities; and thou wilt cast all their sins into the depths of the sea."

Thirdly, God sends our sins to the place of no return, as seen in Psalms 103:12.

Not only does God remit our sins, but he also removes the grip of sin—"He is faithful ... to cleanse us from all unrighteousness."

"Confess" to the Lord and be honest. We must tell God about our sins: private sins (Proverbs 28:13); personal sins (Matthew 5:23–24); and public sins (Matthew 18:15–17).

Allow God to wash you and cleanse you, and then see for yourself that he is a God of second chances. He forgives and forgets as if it didn't happen. Thank God for the blood of Jesus!

Peace,

JTJR

Thank You For Not Leaving Me!

"For thou wilt not leave my soul in hell; neither wilt thou suffer thine Holy One to see corruption." (Psalms 16:10–11)

Take a moment to reflect. Some of us were truly deep in sin! We were rebellious, angry, lustful, and addicted to drugs and alcohol. Some were trapped in sexual immorality. Some went through abuse, rape, betrayal, or just a living hell. But those that have been in the presences of the almighty God Jesus Christ, saved and unsaved, we can all say, "God has saved me from something"! He has gotten us through! God has given us all a chance to know him in a better way! I'm here to encourage all: Jesus will not leave your soul in Hell. Salvation and freedom are available to all who say yes to the Lord and yes to his will.

"Thou wilt shew me the path of life: in thy presence is fulness of joy; at thy right hand there are pleasures for evermore."

Jesus is the way to new life. He won't leave you in your mess; he will wash, restore, and renew you. It's time to live life and live that life more abundantly! I'm grateful that he didn't leave me, and I know he won't leave you!

Love,

JTJR

What's In Your Cup?

Whose cup are you drinking out of? Satan has a cup tailor-made just for us. He has filled it with Patron, Henny, Ciroc, Stella Rose, and Moscato, and he's even added a lemon twist of lies to justify alcohol intake by saying God made water into wine and that Jesus didn't say we can't drink. Out of ignorance, not knowing the text in its proper context, we believe Satan's lies instead of God's truth. Satan has been lying and twisting God's Word since the garden! To the cup, Satan added stress, anxiety, fear, bitterness, unforgiveness, envy, lust, perversion and confusion. There is so much sin and weight in the cup that we have sipped ourselves out of our minds. Being tipsy, buzzed, or drunk is a perfect condition for Satan to devour us. It's time to put that cup down immediately and be sober minded!

There's a cup that's filled with joy, peace, love, grace, mercy, protection, faith—everything we want and need is in this cup! It's tailor-made just for us! The water that was made into wine represented the blood of Jesus. Jesus told the woman at the well that he has living water! The living water is the Holy Ghost. It's time to fill your cup with God himself! Some of us have been dry; some of us need a drink of God. Let

God pour into you. Blessings will continue to flow! Favor will continue to flow; Jesus said it's like rivers of living water! This is your day to say, "My cup runneth over" (Psalms 23:5b). It's time for happy hour and refills are free! Be blessed in Jesus' name.

Love,

JTJR

My Promise Is Bigger Than That

"Behold, I have set the land before you: go in and possess the land which The Lord swear unto fathers ..." (Deuteronomy 1:8a)

I'm here to encourage you to pursue and possess what God has set out for you. He has made promises, he will perform, and he will come through for you. Some of y'all see the promise but haven't possessed it yet. Some haven't possessed it yet because there's some adversity going on. The enemy doesn't want you to have victory. He doesn't want you to prosper in Christ Jesus. Some have fear and doubt. But replace that fear and doubt with faith! Why fear when God's Word is sure? We need to get like Caleb real quick:

"Caleb stilled the people before Moses, and said, Let us go up at once, and possess it; for we are well able to overcome it." (Numbers 13:30–31, 33)

Caleb saw the promise. He was confident, and his faith was in God that they would overcome anything that came up against them!

The Prophet Isaiah said, "No weapon formed against the children of God shall prosper." It's a blessing to have faith, but it's a greater blessing to have a brother or sister in the Lord that has faith in God as well to connect with you.

Caleb was with some busters. Ha, ha. They said, "We be not able to go up against the people; for they are stronger than we. And there we saw the giants, the sons of Anak, which come of the giants: and we were in our own sight as grasshoppers, and so we were in their sight."

Look here: no demon, no devil, no storm, no situation is bigger than God's Word and his promises! He's bigger and greater than that. You need to see yourself as a mighty man or woman of God. You can do all things through Christ who strengthens you. No need to be passive anymore; it's time to go for it! Go for it, because your promise is bigger than your giant situation!

Love,

JTJR

Words With Friends.
Can I Have A Word
With You?

God has something to say to us.

"For my mouth shall speak truth; and wickedness is an abomination to my lips. All the words of my mouth are in righteousness; there is nothing froward or perverse in them." (Proverbs 8:7–8)

The tongue is unruly, laced with poison. The tongue can be disrespectful, abusive, and it can cause death spiritually, emotionally, financially, mentally, and physically. Relationships of all types, families, businesses, dreams, and visions have all been destroyed because of a froward, perverted, lying mouth! Satan lied to Eve in the garden; she was deceived, and we're in the mess that we are now because she believed a lie instead of truth!

Many join cults, gangs, follow trends, and personalities that are cunning and ungodly. Satan knows how to make it look good and sound good. He has game, so don't you fool yourself. We must be careful that wickedness not be in our mouths! It's an abomination to our lips!

Our mouths should be filled with love, joy, peace, and the Word of God who is Jesus Christ. Praise and thanksgiving should be in our mouths! Truth and righteousness ought to be in our mouths! Speak the truth in love. Sugar coat nothing, but speak with grace, love, and wisdom. Know when to speak and when to shut up. Enough with the subliminal messages, and enough with the gossip! Every idle word is being accounted; according to God, we are justified and condemned by the words of our mouths! Watch your mouth, change your language and speak the words of life and truth in Christ Jesus.

Love,

√TᵥR

How Do You See Yourself?

"And there we saw the giants, the sons of Anak, which come of the giants: and we were in our own sight as grasshoppers, and so we were in their sight." (Numbers 13:33 KJV)

Ladies and gents, we ought to see ourselves as royalty. We are kings and queens. God made us after his image and likeness. But Satan is a deceiver, he is a liar, and he has tainted and polluted this world. For many of us, it's hard to see ourselves in the way God intended for us to be. Satan had many of us out there wild 'n out. Some men are trying to be women and some women are trying to be men. We have women calling themselves the "Baddest B" or a "Good B." Some men think they are pimps and players. Satan has this generation so perverted, lustful, and full of drugs and alcohol, but they see nothing wrong with it! The devil is a liar, and we rebuke every foul spirit in Jesus' name! We must understand that we are bigger, better, and brighter than the picture Satan has set out. We must understand and realize the Greater One within us. We are stronger and greater than any giant because Christ Jesus lives within us. For it's in him we live, move, and have our being! Change your perspective on life and see God within yourself. Pray, praise, and worship till you see God manifest in your life and others. You're much more than a grasshopper. We are a child of the King, King Jesus! I hope you can see yourself better now; I hope you can see Christ in you now!

Love,

JTJR

The Struggle Is Real, But...

Apostle Paul stated in Romans Chapter 7, "... when I would do good evil is present ..."

We pray, fast, and seek God's Word, but the devil likes to show his head. Sometimes life's trials seem unbearable and our flesh gets to talking and wants its sinful appetites to be fed; we find ourselves discouraged, in sin, backslidden and out of God's will. Yes, the struggle is real, but God said, "do not throw away your confidence; it will be richly rewarded."

It's easy to give up and to do so quickly. Try to trust God, keep your faith, and trust in Jesus no matter what. If we suffer with Christ, we will reign with him. When the devil gets to talking, speak the Word against him, and when your flesh starts talking, decrease so God will increase in you.

God said, "You need to persevere so that when you have done the will of God, you will receive what he has promised."

God's will is perfect for us. We can rejoice in the Lord, for he is our strength. He can't lie and his

Word and his promises will come to pass. The struggle is real, but the reward is so much greater!

Love you all,

JTJR

JOHN THOMAS JR.

GET YOUR BREAD UP

"Give us this day our daily bread." (Matthew 6:11)

It's amazing how we will work 40–50 hours a week, sometimes weekends, sick or in health, for money but can't spend two hours in church with God on a Sunday morning. We can't spend an hour in Bible class, yet we say "TGIF."

It's amazing how some folk won't talk to you unless you look like a million bucks. There's a YG song called "You Broke" that says, "Shut up / Don't talk to me / Get your bread up".

This is the mentality of our world.

I'm all for getting bread (money) daily, and I'm all for nice things, but what does it profit a man to gain the world and *lose* his *soul?* Is your job more important than God? Many get up early to be at work on time but can't get out of bed for Jesus, who is our Lord and Savior? Jesus is the *bread of life.* The daily bread we ought to be getting is the Word of God! The Word of God washes us, heals us, saves us, delivers us, and strengthens us. Daily, we need bread so we can fight against the devil and his demons. We need more bread, more of Jesus, than anything right now in our world. Greed has killed our economy, and we are at war and in other countries over money! Our children are being indoctrinated with perversion morally, mentally, emotionally, and spiritually. We need to get more bread in our children and this generation. We need every bit of God!

Make it your business to get your bread up. Stay prayed up, stay in your Word in your private time, get in Bible class and Sunday school, and be in service on Sunday morning so the Sheppard can teach you and explain the Word in a more excellent way! This is the time to get your bread up!

Love,

√T√R

I'm Not Trying To Hear It! Kill The Noise!

"But shun profane and vain babblings: for they will increase unto more ungodliness." (2 Timothy 2:16)

Faith cometh by hearing and hearing the Word of God. When God speaks, we must take heed to his Word. We don't have time for lies and broken promises. Innocent people have been hurt, locked up, and killed over lies. Broken promises have shattered people's faith, and it's by faith that we please God! Let's be real: we don't have time for the foolishness, and God said to shun profane and vain babblings.

Just tell me what God said. Jesus said we are the head and not the tail. Jesus said that no weapon formed against us shall prosper. Jesus said stand still and see the salvation of the Lord. Jesus said it's his good pleasure to bless us. Jesus said greater is he that is within us than he that's in the world! It's time for us to kill the noise of the world and hear from God Almighty! If it's not God's Word, I don't want to hear it!

Word up.

JTJR

The Lord Will Do Wonders

"Joshua said unto the people, Sanctify yourselves: for tomorrow the Lord will do wonders among you." (Joshua 3:5–7, 10–11, 17)

God is about to do *wonders* in our lives. But before we dance and before we get too happy, we must sanctify ourselves. That part right there is a deal breaker for some. Sanctify means to be set apart, consecrated and holy. We must decrease first so God can increase! This means we have to get rid of the dead weight and sins that easily beset us. Remember though, God will do wonders! God can't lie so do what needs to be done: Put the blunt and the cigs out! Get some water, Kool-Aid, or juice, and leave the alcohol alone! This is not the time to be bitter, envious, unforgiving, lustful or prideful. We know the things that easily beset us. But as we sanctify ourselves, repent, pray, praise, worship, and seek God and his Word, the anointing of God will strengthen and keep us!

Joshua and the children of Israel had enemies they had to face, they had a Jordan River they had to cross, no matter what we are facing and dealing with, God said, "Tomorrow I shall do wonders"!

Just like Joshua and the children of Israel, we have the Word of God, and the Ark of the Covenant shall go before the people.

And God said, "Without fail drive out from before you the Canaanites, and the Hittites, and the Hivites, and the Perizzites, and the Girgashites, and the Amorites, and the Jebusites."

God is going to drive your enemies, struggles, and burdens out! We shall cross the Jordan River! No matter what you face, God is making a clear path for a smooth landing!

I encourage all to be sanctified now! Miracles, signs, and wonders will take place in your life now. The scripture said tomorrow, but we serve an eternal God. Your tomorrow can be today! Your tomorrow can be right now. It could be the 23rd in the States, but in other countries it's already the 24th! I dare you to sanctify yourself and see the blessings and wonders of the Lord overtake you now in Jesus' name!

May the Lord bless you now!

Love,

JTJR

I'm Anointed For This!
I Will Fight For You!

To every blood-washed, redeemed, Holy Ghost–filled, water- and fire-baptized believer, *you have the victory*! I don't know what you're facing, but God tells us throughout scripture, "Fear not, stand still and see the salvation of the Lord." Satan walks to and fro, seeking whom he may devour. He's out to kill, steal, and destroy, but thanks be unto God who giveth us the victory! Before the battle, God has already anointed us! David was anointed king before time. Before we were formed in our mothers' wombs, God had already sanctified and ordained us!

So when Goliath showed up, David was ready!

"And David said to Saul, Let no man's heart fail because of him; thy servant will go and fight with this Philistine. And Saul said to David, Thou art not able to go against this Philistine to fight with him: for thou art but a youth, and he a man of war from his youth." (1 Samuel 17:32–33)

Saul didn't know what he was talking about! He didn't even know what David had gone through! There are some folk who will count you out because of your age. But I can hear Apostle Paul say, "Let no man despise thy youth".

Everybody has a testimony! We have some folk who've gone through molestation, rape, drug abuse, shootings, stabbings, abandonment, etc., but God has kept each and every one, saved each and every one, and filled them with the power of the Holy Ghost and gladness by serving the Lord! We have young people who fast, pray, seek God, and worship him in spirit and truth and are well-able to pull down strongholds and wicked imaginations.

David testified to the king and said in 1 Samuel 17:34–37, "… a lion, and a bear, took a lamb out of the flock: And I went after him … slew both the lion and the bear: And this uncircumcised Philistine shall be as one of them, seeing he hath defied the armies of the living God." David's faith was so high he said, "The Lord that delivered me out of the paw of the lion, and out of the paw of the bear, he will deliver me out of the hand of this Philistine."

Saul was the king, and he was scared to fight. Some of our parents and grandparents didn't kill the generational curses in our families, but we need to get like David and kill every generational curse in our families. Enough is enough: Fight for your family; fight for your friends; attack and kill that molestation and rape demon; attack and kill that homosexual and lesbian spirit; and attack and kill that lying, violent, abusive drug and alcohol spirit in the name of Jesus! You know the things going on, so call those demons out, bind them in the name of Jesus! War in the Spirit and watch deliverance take place! You have the power of thee anointing and God on your side! We have the *victory* in the name of Jesus Christ! It's time to go to war!

Love,

√T√R

Leave That Ass Alone

"Thou shalt not plow with an ox and an ass to-gether." (Deuteronomy 22:10)

Ox: The ox is considered to be a tolerant, courageous, hard-working, strong animal.

Ass: The ass is a dull, heavy, stupid fellow, a dolt.

The reason why God commanded us not to plow, work, or yoke an ox and ass together is because they're not compatible. As we can see, an ox is about business, courage, and strength. An ass is lazy, lifeless, and stupid.

The reason why many aren't being blessed and getting all that God has for them is because they are hooked up to too many asses! To my brothers who are saved to the bone and living for Jesus, I don't care if she looks like Beyoncé, and paid like her; if she isn't saved, sanctified, Holy Ghost–filled, fire- and water-baptized in *Jesus' name*, then leave that ass alone! Don't you yoke up with her. She will have your feelings going crazy, and she could be Delilah under that MAC makeup, ready to destroy you! There was a young man that killed himself over a girl named

"Honey Cocaine." Man, please; the devil is a lie! Honey Cocaine? Brothers, please understand who you are in Christ Jesus and know that no good thing will God keep from you! You are a king and God has a queen just for you!

Sisters, y'all too; I don't care if he looks like Chris Brown, muscle bound and chocolate like Morris Chestnut; if he doesn't love God, if he's not following Christ, leave that ass alone! No sense in you trying to get his attention! No sense in you crying over somebody that isn't trying to be the shadow of Jesus Christ! God will send his son, and there is a king in every son of God; he's just for you! Wait on the Lord, ladies and gents!

We have family, friends, and even associates in business in our lives who are lazy, doing stupid stuff, and always looking for a handout. Yes, we love them, but leave that ass alone! Encourage them to become an *ox*!

We must be careful of our own activities and habits. It's cool to go out and have fun, but if going out is taking up your prayer and study time with God, you have to leave it alone! Smoking, drinking, fornicating—things that are not of God will have us unproductive, unfruitful, and yup, we look and feel like an ass.

We must be sanctified, set apart, renewed and refreshed daily in Christ Jesus. God through Apostle Paul told us,

"And what concord hath Christ with Belial? or what part hath he that believeth with an infidel? And what agreement hath the temple of God with idols? for ye are the temple of the living God; as God hath said, I will dwell in them, and walk in them; and I will be their God, and they shall be my people. Wherefore come out from among them, and be ye separate, saith the Lord, and touch not the unclean thing; and I will receive you, And will be a Father unto you, and ye shall be my sons and daughters, saith the Lord Almighty." (II Corinthians 6:14–18)

All of us need to examine ourselves, laying aside every weight and sin that easily beset us. When we do so, God will receive us and we will receive what God has for us! God has blessed us and has commanded us in this life to be fruitful, multiply and replenish the earth (Genesis 1:28). This is our season to be fruitful, multiply, and replenish. It's time to be that ox and leave the asses alone!

Love,

JTJR

MY PRAISE BELONGS TO GOD

"And David danced before the Lord with all his might and David was girded with a linen ephod. So David and all the house of Israel brought up the Ark of the Lord with shouting and with the sound of the trumpet. And as the Ark of the Lord came in the city of David Michal Saul's daughter looked through a window and saw King David leaping and dancing before the Lord and she despised him in her heart. Then David returned to bless his household, and Michal the Daughter of Saul came out to meet David, and said how glorious was the king of Israel today, who uncovered himself today in the eyes of the handmaids of his servants as one of the vain fellows shamelessly uncovereth himself! And David said unto Michal it was before the Lord which chose me before thy father and before all his house to appoint me ruler over the people of the Lord over Israel therefore will I play before the Lord. Therefore Michal the Daughter of Saul had no child unto the day of her death." (II Samuel 6:14–16, 20–21, 23)

The Ark is called the "strength and the glory of God," and it also represented the Word of God. We know that Jesus is the Word, and we ought to thank God that he is our strength. We should understand King David's excitement. There's nothing like having God in your heart, mind, body, soul, and spirit. There's nothing like the glory of God filling the temple. The Word of the Lord said, "In his presence there's fullness of Joy and at his right hand pleasures for evermore." Bishop Hezekiah Walker has a song called "Every Praise," and every praise belongs to our God! He is and has been so amazing to us all; we owe the Lord some praise.

It's a shame that David's wife despised him and didn't like how he gave God glory in the manner he did. I can hear Bishop Larry D. Trotter say, "You don't know my story, and all the things that I've been through; you can't feel my pain, what I had to go through to get here. You will never understand my praise. Don't try to figure it out because *my worship is for real.*"

Please believe, saints of God, we have the right and a reason to praise the Lord!

Look here, don't link up with a non-praiser. The Lord lives in the midst of praise! We need to be where the Lord is and dwells daily. Praise confuses the enemy. Praise will make you feel better. Praise will cause your situation to be better. Praise is to be continuous, and anybody that hates and despise your praise and worship just might be on the path to being cursed just like Michal. Don't mind the haters; continue to praise and worship the Lord, because all praise belongs to God!

Love,

JTJR

Touch Him With Your Greater Faith

"And saying, Lord, my servant lieth at home sick of the palsy, grievously tormented. And Jesus saith unto him, I will come and heal him. The centurion answered and said, Lord, I am not worthy that thou shouldest come under my roof: but speak the word only, and my servant shall be healed." (Matthew 8:6–8)

This story is so powerful that we all can relate some way or another. There are so many people who believe that Jesus is God. They know he saves and delivers. They know Jesus is the blesser, but because of how they are living, they don't believe they can be blessed. Many feel like they have to get it right first before they can come to Jesus. But that's not the case. We all have done something wrong, but thank God for Calvary! Thank God that we can call on the name of Jesus. Thank God we can call on that name that still saves, heals, delivers, and sets free. There's salvation in the name of Jesus. The name of the Lord is a strong tower, and the righteous run into it and are safe! Never be afraid to call on his name!

As we read this story we really don't know why this man didn't want Jesus to come under his roof. But it's a blessing that this man came to Jesus, and the Lord showed compassion, grace, and mercy towards him! Thank God we serve a God of compassion.

The very thing that touched Jesus was this man's faith. For the scripture said without faith it is impossible to please the Lord. This centurion asked Jesus to just speak the word, and he believed that when Jesus spoke the word his servant would be healed.

This man had no doubt that Jesus saves. Who knows, this man could have heard something about Jesus. For we know that faith cometh by hearing and hearing the Word of God. This man could have heard that Jesus turned water into wine. He could have heard that Jesus laid hands on the sick and they recovered. This man could have heard the great things that God has done. Saints of God, we must tell our stories and tell the goodness of Jesus and what he has done for us in our lives.

Jesus is all-knowing, all-powerful, and our God is full of compassion and love, so when this man came running to Jesus and told him his story about his sick servant, Jesus let it be known that he had his back. Please believe God has our back as well. For the things that seem impossible, he's going to do something that will blow our minds. Our God is awesome like that. Jesus said in verse 10 of Matthew 8,

*"When Jesus heard it, he marvelled, and said to
them that followed, Verily I say unto you, I have
not found so great faith, no, not in Israel."*

This is crazy ... Jesus said to his own disciples that
he hadn't found so great faith in all of Israel! The
people that followed Jesus, that got the word and
walked with the word every day, didn't have faith
like this unworthy man!

Saints of God, don't allow somebody that doesn't
even follow Jesus to have more Faith than you. This
man didn't follow Jesus, but he had heard about
him. He felt like he wasn't even worthy to have God
Almighty walk in his house, but he simply asked
Jesus to speak the word that his servant would be
healed. This man touched Jesus through his faith!

We must learn how to touch Jesus the right way!

*"And Jesus said unto the centurion, Go thy way;
and as thou hast believed, so be it done unto thee.
And his servant was healed in the selfsame hour."
(Matthew 8:13)*

Our God is faithful, he is just, and he is true; he
loves us and he has compassion for us. This same
God that came through for the sick servant and the
centurion will come through for you if you believe!
Whatever you want, whatever you need from the

Lord, it's yours for the asking. All we must do is come to God with a humble heart, a humble spirit; be real, don't be fake with it, tell the Lord your problems, tell him your situation, bring all your burdens to the Lord, and then leave it in God's hands! Tap into your faith and watch God show up in your situation. God has spoken his word over your life. Tap into your greater faith; "faith is the substance of things hoped for, the evidence of things not seen."

I dare you to activate your faith.

Love,

JTJR

Lord Keep Me In Your Hands

"The steps of a good man are ordered by the LORD: and he delighteth in his way. Though he fall, he shall not be utterly cast down: for the LORD upholdeth him with his hand." (Psalms 37:23–24)

When we say yes to God, our worldly desires change. We begin to have a hunger and thirst for righteousness. We decrease so God can increase in us. We abide in him and he will abide in us. When we walk and live in divine order, we delight in God's will. Our God is awesome and all-knowing; he knows we may fall short at times. The scripture goes on to say, "Though he fall, he shall not be utterly cast down: for the LORD upholdeth him with his hand."

Though we mess up, though we fall, we are not going to stay down forever! God has already given us the victory in Christ Jesus. We have the blood of Jesus on our side. We have grace and mercy. God is faithful and just to cleanse us from all unrighteousness! God will help us to overcome, because he said, "the Lord upholdeth [us] with his hand." It's with that same hand that he blessed us. It's with that same hand that he protects us, and it's with that same hand that he bears the scars which should be on our hands. It's that same hand that blood came out of when they nailed him to the cross. It was that same hand that Thomas touched and believed! It's that same hand that will lift us up!

There may be times when we feel like we have been handed over to men, like trouble is all around us, like God isn't around, like we have no hope, like men try to cast us down and bring us down, but thanks be unto God that he made a covenant with us. God inscribed us in his hand. When we get baptized in Jesus' name and filled with the Holy Ghost, we are then called his sons and daughters. What real father would leave his child down and out? King David said, "I have been young, and now am old; yet have I not seen the righteous forsaken, nor his seed begging bread." Know that Jesus is there always! The eyes of the Lord are everywhere. Know that Jesus has us on his mind! God is so awesome and so much better than man that God looks beyond our faults. Know that Jesus has us in his hands!

Love,

JTJR

Leave It To God

"So God created man in his own image, in the image of God created he him; male and female created he them. And God saw everything that he had made, and, behold, it was very good. And the evening and the morning were the sixth day."
(Genesis 1:27, 31)

We live in a day and time where some men want a woman looking like a supermodel, built like Beyoncé, blessed from top to the "Apple Bottom," educated, independent, submissive, ride-or-die, a freak in the sheets, etc. Some modern-day women want a man who is tall, dark, and handsome with tats; who's gangsta, sweet, but loves God too; who can party and drink a little bit; yet have goals, ambitions, etc. There's nothing wrong with knowing what you like, but some of the things we like aren't good for us! God knows what we want and what we need. The devil knows what we want and what we don't need, and he will try to give us what we don't need. And if the devil can help us create what we want, it's going to be all bad. Many people right now are creating monsters. I mean, really love God but still live a life of sin?

Many women today, because of what they created in their minds and flesh, have been abused physically, mentally, spiritually, and financially. Many have been turned out and strung out on drugs, alcohol, and perversion. Ladies, be careful what you ask for without doing a deeper search of all that comes with the package deal. Be careful about what you ask for and create in your mind. It's sad because some women are so wounded that they start seeking the same sex.

Many men have fallen and picked the wrong woman. Samson was picking the wrong ones all his life. He was married before and now he falls in love with a harlot named Delilah. She was in it for money! Be careful of those gold diggers, fellas.

We need to wake up and do a quick examination of what we truly want and need! Stop looking at the outward appearance and look at the heart! We have to do away with the flesh-mates and allow God to bless us with a soul-mate. God has nothing but good gifts for us. And no good thing will he withhold from us.

It's time for those who are single to seek the Lord and allow God to bring you your wife or your husband. It's time to set your criteria on the level of holiness, on the level where God wants you to be!

We've done enough damage. Let's leave it to God; he knows what's best.

Love,

JTJR

Precious

"When they went from one nation to another, from one kingdom to another people; He suffered no man to do them wrong: yea, he reproved kings for their sakes; Saying, Touch not mine anointed, and do my prophets no harm." (Psalms 105:13–15)

"As a child of the King we are Precious in his sight. The Question was asked 'What is man that art mindful of him?'"

God has been faithful to us even when we were faithless. The word of the Lord said while we were yet sinners, while we were yet hurting God's feelings and breaking his heart, while we were drunk, high, fornicating, committing adultery, lying, cheating, abusing ourselves, living a sodomite lifestyle, and doing everything ungodly, God took it upon himself, upon his hands, and he was nailed to the cross for our sins. Jesus did all this for us because he knew that we were in need of a savior, a second chance, and he knew that we are precious.

Because of God's grace, his mercy, and his blood, which was shed, he gave us a chance to be saved and to be filled with the Holy Ghost. And many of us have been born again. We have received Christ as Lord, we have repented of our sins, we have been baptized in Jesus' name, and we have been filled with the Holy Ghost. Now we are sons and daughters of the Most High God. We are the righteousness of God in Christ Jesus. We need to know that we are special; we are precious!

The word of the Lord in verse 15 reminded us and others to touch not God's anointed and do them, the prophet no harm. We need to be careful and handle God's people with care and with gtrace. When we go to the post office and we want to deliver a package, we have the choice to label our package as fragile and to handle with care. We have been labeled, we have been bought with a price, we belong to God, and we need to be handled with care. We also need to love and care for our brothers and sisters in Christ.

It's time to know who we are in Christ Jesus. We are precious. We are kings and queens. We are a holy nation; we are a royal priesthood; we are a peculiar people. We are the sons and daughters of the Most High God Jesus Christ. We are precious. We need to love one another, care for one another, and pray for one another. Rebuke in love. Lift one another up. We need to stand in the gap for one another. Encourage your mother, father, sister, brother—encourage the church of Jesus Christ. God said the thoughts that he thinks towards us are of peace, of good and not of evil. God has great things in store for his people. We are special, we are precious, and there is a brighter day coming. Hold your head up high, and know that the King of Glory is coming in your life; he is coming in your situation and breakthroughs are happening even now. You are not a failure, and you are not lazy. Don't let the world dictate anything, and don't let the devil dictate anything or call you anything. God has called you Barak. Barak is a Hebrew word which means blessed! You are blessed! And before this year is out, God is going to show himself strong in your life, because you are precious and he cares about you; so do I!

Love,

JTJR

Where Will You Be Found?

I have a few questions, and I'm sure everybody will agree with this assessment.

If someone drinks alcohol a lot, where can they be found? I would think the corner store, the liquor store, wines and spirits. If someone smokes all the time, they are found at the weed man's house, the smoke shop getting blunts, getting cigars or cigarettes. If someone loves to party and dance, they are usually found in the clubs or at somebody's party going ham on the dance floor.

In my opinion, it makes sense. So let me ask this question: Where is the Christian? Where should the saints of the Most High be found? Jesus is our perfect example, so let's see where he was found.

> "And when he was twelve years old, they went up to Jerusalem after the custom of the feast. And when they had fulfilled the days, as they returned, the child Jesus tarried behind in Jerusalem; and Joseph and his mother knew not of it. But they, supposing him to have been in the company, went a day's journey; and they sought him among their kinsfolk and acquaintance. And when they found him not, they turned back again to Jerusalem,

seeking him. And it came to pass, that after three days they found him in the temple, sitting in the midst of the doctors, both hearing them, and asking them questions." (Luke 2:42–46)

Somehow, some way, Mary and Joseph left Jesus in Jerusalem, and they had to go back to find him. They found Jesus in the temple sitting in the midst of the doctors, listening and asking questions.

The Word goes on to tell us in Luke 2:47–49,

"And all that heard him were astonished at his understanding and answers. And when they saw him, they were amazed: and his mother said unto him, Son, why hast thou thus dealt with us? behold, thy father and I have sought thee sorrowing. And he said unto them, How is it that ye sought me? wist ye not that I must be about my Father's business?"

Those that were in the temple couldn't believe the wisdom and the knowledge that this young boy had. Even when his parents came into the church house, they were amazed of what they saw and what they heard coming from their child's mouth. People should be amazed when they see you working in the church. They should be amazed to see you praying and lifting up the name of Jesus. Some should be amazed because they remember when you were lost, but thank Jesus for salvation! As Christians we ought to be found in *church*!

The Word of the Lord already told us to forsake not the assemblies of the saints together. A true Christian will be found in the house of the Lord. Jesus was found in the house of the Lord. Then he had holy boldness and said, "I'm about my father's business." Are you about your heavenly Father's business? Can your friends and family actually say you're always in church, you're always in prayer, you're always giving in the offering plate, you're always praying, you're always on a fast, you're always leaping for joy, you're always getting loud praising God? Can anyone say that about you? Can they truly find you to be faithful in the service of the Lord?

Saints of God, let's be where God wants us to be. Let's be found in Christ and doing Kingdom work.

Love,

JTJR

Don't Seek a Sign But A Word And The Sign Will Follow You

"And it came to pass, as he spake these things, a certain woman of the company lifted up her voice, and said unto him, Blessed is the womb that bare thee, and the paps which thou hast sucked. But he said, Yea rather, blessed are they that hear the word of God, and keep it. And when the people were gathered thick together, he began to say, This is an evil generation: they seek a sign; and there shall no sign be given it, but the sign of Jonas the prophet. For as Jonas was a sign unto the Ninevites, so shall also the Son of man be to this generation." (Luke 11:27–30)

We live in a day when people will look up their zodiac sign to get a sign or a word for their day. We even have people who won't date you if you're not the right sign! Some people rely on their sign and zodiac word instead of picking up their Bibles and getting direction, wisdom, and knowledge from God Almighty. Jesus even got upset in Mark Chapter 8:12:

"And he sighed deeply in his spirit, and saith, Why doth this generation seek after a sign? verily I say unto you, There shall no sign be given unto this generation."

I want everyone reading this to know that they should not waste time looking for a sign because no sign will be given. However, Jesus will always give a Word. God wants us to seek him. In the text of Luke, Jesus said unto the woman like he is saying to us, "Blessed are they that hear the word of God, and keep it." When you get a Word from the Lord and receive it in faith and in confidence, he will bring it to pass. Jesus has spoken a Word to each and every one of us. Jesus said blessed are they that hear the word, but not only hear it—keep it.

We need to seek the Word of God. We need to trust the Lord. We need to believe in him. Once we do this, God will manifest his glory in our lives. And because of the Word, the sign is now following us. Mark 16:17-18 said, "And these signs shall follow them that believe; in my name they shall cast out devils."

"They shall lay hands on the sick, and they shall recover." But this will happen only through his Word. We don't need a sign to get a miracle; we have the Word to do a miracle! The power and the authority is in the Word of God. The power is in your faith—to believe and keep it in your heart, mind, and spirit.

God is able to do exceedingly, abundantly above all that we can ask or think according to the power that worketh in us! It's up to us to seek the Lord. It's up to us to seek his Word, trust in him, and he will give us what we need.

Family, don't search for signs anymore. For the wicked seek out signs and they won't get one. But those who are King's kids who seek the Lord, seek his Word, and trust in him—the signs will follow you because the glory will be manifested in your life.

Love,

√T√R

God Save The King And Queen

"And when Athaliah the mother of Ahaziah saw that her son was dead, she arose and destroyed all the seed royal. But Jehosheba, the daughter of king Joram, sister of Ahaziah, took Joash the son of Ahaziah, and stole him from among the king's sons which were slain; and they hid him, even him and his nurse, in the bedchamber from Athaliah, so that he was not slain. And he was with her hid in the house of the LORD six years. And Athaliah did reign over the land." (2 Kings 11:1–3, 12)

Athaliah was an evil grandmother who wanted to be a ruler and be in charge over Judah. The only way that was going to happen: She had to kill the baby boys in line to be king. Please understand that there are some people in your life and even in your family that don't want you to reach your destiny. They don't want to see you blessed. There are some people that want to kill your dreams. You can't tell everybody your dreams and goals. You can't tell everybody what God has spoken to you.

This grandmother wasn't that smart. She didn't know all of her grandkids. The kings in those days always had other wives and they had kids. The step-sister, if you want to call it that, Jehosheba the sister of Ahaziah took her little nephew and hid him in the house of the Lord for six years. Please understand there is safety in the house of the Lord. Because they raised this young child in the house of the Lord for six years, in those six years they were preparing him for kingship. They were teaching him. He was getting his education and wisdom right there in the house of the Lord.

Whatever you need, God has it in the house! A lot of people lack wisdom and understanding; that's because they don't want to be taught. They don't want to learn, nor do they want to hear. And God told us in Hosea, "Our people are destroyed for the lack of knowledge." But he that hath an ear to hear let him hear what the spirit hath to say. For faith cometh by hearing and hearing the word of God, this young man was in the house getting it all at a young age! Sit those kids down and teach them about Jesus. Bring them to church. Thank God for this auntie that took this young king to the house of the Lord and kept him there. While his evil grandmother was ruling the land, this young boy was preparing for the next level.

"And he brought forth the king's son, and put the crown upon him, and gave him the testimony; and they made him king, and anointed him; and they clapped their hands, and said, God save the king." (2 Kings 11:1–3, 12)

To those who were in the temple, those who were training this young man in the house of the Lord, it was time for him to be king. They crowned him, they told him everything that was going on in the land, they told him what his grandmother did to his brothers, they told him about the false gods that his grandmother had the land worshiping—oh yeah, they told the story. Then they made him king and anointed him. Then they rejoiced and clapped their hands because they knew that the hand of the Lord was on him! God saved the King.

Have you ever wondered why God saved you? Have you ever wondered why God kept you when everybody was getting shot and killed all around you and bullets just passed you? I was out with my friend Twan for his birthday one night. We had a great time. We planned to go to Denny's and we all took different cars. Twan and the rest of the guys left before me. As I was driving I saw the car they were in crashed on the side of the road. The accident was caused by gun shots. The bullet hit his leg but didn't penetrate. It just fell off his leg! God stopped that bullet!

While we were getting high, getting drunk, jumping from one bed to the next, sleeping with this dude and that girl and even the same sex, God spared us! Have you ever wonder why God kept you through all the hellish things you have done when the wages of sin is death? We knew we should have been dead already, but God kept us. It's not because we are lucky and it's not because we got it like that; it's because of the blood of Jesus and his grace, and he has a plan for our lives. We have been anointed king and queen!

Somebody in our family from generations back has prayed for us! Just like Joash's auntie—she knew that if she could get her nephew to church and introduce him to Jesus, everything would be alright! Family, we have been anointed *king and queen*! For we are a royal priesthood, a holy nation, a peculiar people. Jesus had us on his mind, for the thoughts he thinks towards us are of good and of peace and not of evil! God has a plan for your life!

The text goes on to tell us not only did Joash reign over the land, but he also brought the true and living God back in the land! Not only did he put his grandmother to death, but also everyone that tainted the house of the Lord. Joash brought order back to the house of God.

I encourage everyone to stay in the house of God. Don't compromise the Gospel of Jesus Christ. It's still holiness. The steps of a good man are ordered by the Lord. Let us follow Jesus, let us walk with him, and just like Joash, we shall have favor with the Lord.

I'm so glad that Jesus made me king. God has saved the king and queen!

DO YOU UNDERSTAND?

In life, growing up, and being in a couple of relationships, this phrase has come up: "Do you understand?" We could do something wrong or something can be explained, and the question may come up: Do you understand? And if we are honest, we didn't understand all the time what our parents were trying to tell us and teach us. We don't understand what our spouses were trying to tell us all the time. But in order to understand, anything, we must be taught, we must have information, and we must be instructed.

"Hear, ye children, the instruction of a father, and attend to know understanding. For I give you good doctrine, forsake ye not my law. For I was my father's son, tender and only beloved in the sight of my mother. He taught me also, and said unto me, Let thine heart retain my words: keep my commandments, and live."(Proverbs 4:1–7)

It's a blessing in the natural to have a father in your life. A father to teach his children, to lead them, and guide them through life the best way he knows how. Jesus is our spiritual and Heavenly Father. For Jesus is the way, the truth, and the life. As he speaks to us he says, "Hear ye children the instructions of a father" (natural father, pastor, bishop, etc.). He that has an ear to hear let him hear what the spirit has to say. Be tentative to know understanding. For Jesus has given us good doctrine. Let us hold on to the Word of God and sound doctrine. We must know the Word of God; we must know the sound doctrine of Jesus Christ. But in order to know it, the head, the leader, the father must preach it and teach it! There's only one Gospel. But some of these leaders, preachers, and teachers are not preaching sound doctrine, and because of that we have weak saints, weakness in some churches, and when the truth is really preached and taught, some won't even be able to endure it. That's because the head that they sit under didn't give them the proper instructions. But it's our job, those who are born again, to teach and instruct many (Daniel 11:33)!

Those who are truly seeking God and seeking for more, there is a word for you:

"Get wisdom, get understanding: forget it not; neither decline from the words of my mouth. Forsake her not, and she shall preserve thee: love her, and she shall keep thee. Wisdom is the principal thing; therefore get wisdom: and with all thy getting get understanding." (Proverbs 4:5–7)

God said get wisdom, get understanding, in all thy getting get an understanding. Wisdom and knowledge is there for the asking (James 1:5). God wants us to be smart; God wants us to be like him. Many quote the scripture: "His way is not our ways, his thoughts are not our thoughts." But if we actually read Isaiah 55 all the way through, the wicked weren't trying to walk in God's way and God was like, "forget them"; let the wicked forsake his way, but whoever wants to follow Jesus, he will have mercy on them.

The wicked ways are not his ways; God's thoughts are not their thoughts. In the New Testament the question was asked, "Who hath the mind of Christ?" Those who have been born again, let this mind be in you which is in Christ Jesus! We need to be renewed in our minds! We don't need to have a carnal mind but have a spiritual mind! Be not conformed to this world but be ye transformed by the renewing of your mind. Change the way you think; have the mind of Christ. Have the spirit of God in you, for the spirit searches the deep things. There are some things you might not understand but lean not to thy own understanding; trust the Lord, acknowledge him, and he will direct your path. We need to have a hunger and a thirst for righteousness. We need to have a hunger and thirst for his Word. We need more of his Word. We don't need to wonder anymore; we need a word from the Lord. And God will fill us with his Word and we shall be satisfied.

In order to understand we must study. Don't just read, but study and meditate on God's Word. God will reveal if we truly consecrate ourselves. Fast, pray, praise, worship, go to church faithfully, get under leadership that's going to preach and teach *all* of his Word. Be under leadership where Jesus will be preached. Be under leadership where sound and good doctrine is taught. And when you do so, you will truly understand. This is the Word of the Lord concerning you.

Love,

JTJR

We Can't Act Like Them

"Ye shall therefore keep all my statutes, and all my judgments, and do them: That the land, whither I bring you to dwell therein, spue you not out. And ye shall not walk in the manners of the nation, which I cast out before you: for they committed all these things, and therefore I abhorred them."
(Leviticus 20:22–26)

The Word of the Lord declared to us to keep all his Word, all of his statutes and all of his judgment. Not only should we keep his Word and his judgments but also do them as well. Jesus said, "Not only be hearers of the word but be ye also doers of the word." King David through God said, "He that Dwelleth in the secret place of the most high shall abide under the shadow of the Almighty." Jesus said, "If you abide in me I will abide in you." Jesus also reminded us to be holy for he is holy.

Why must we be in our Word? Why must we allow the Word to abide in us, why must we live holy? Because where God is taking us, it requires a higher level of anointing and faith. The blessing that God has in store for us, the very things God has promised—they will come to pass, but first we must decrease that he may increase. We have some deadweight in our lives, Some sins that are holding up our promises and blessings. But just like God did for Israel, he will do for us; he is going to deliver us only if we allow him to.

Jesus gave Israel instructions. He said don't walk in the same manner as the nations which he is casting out for they have committed some hellish sins. God said that the sins, the things they are doing, are abhorred, which means disgusting.

The things our nations are doing are horrible and disgusting. We have a nation where men want to marry men. We have a nation where children are being disobedience to parents. We have a nation where people are raping young girls and boys. We have people committing hellish murders and doing drive-by shootings. We have a nation that will party hard, drink all night, and smoke all day. We have a nation where the love is waxed cold, no care for nobody! And now these spirits have even crept in the church. People have no respect for God or his house. Some don't even go to the house on a regular; they will even tell you, "I don't have to go to church every day or every Sunday and I'll still be saved." But Jesus told us in his Word, "Forsake not the assemblies of the saints together"! But those who act like that are casual Christians. They don't have a true relationship with the Lord, because the Lord was always found in the temple. Those who have a true relationship, those who are truly saved and filled with the Holy Ghost— we know where to be, and God said don't even follow them, don't even walk in their manner. We can't act like them, for we have a promise.

> *"But I have said unto you, Ye shall inherit their land, and I will give it unto you to possess it, a land that floweth with milk and honey: I am the LORD your God, which have separated you from other people. Ye shall therefore put difference between clean beasts and unclean, and between unclean fowls and clean: and ye shall not make your souls abominable by beast, or by fowl, or by any manner of living thing that creepeth on the ground, which I have separated from you as unclean. And ye shall be holy unto me: for I the LORD am holy, and have severed you from other people, that ye should be mine."*
> *(Leviticus 20:22–26)*

Jesus has an abundance of blessings for us, Jesus has already spoken unto us, Jesus has greater for us that we shall inherit, and Jesus said he will give it to us to possess it for he is the Lord our God! But in order to get this blessing, we must separate ourselves. One scripture said, "If my people which are called by my name shall humble themselves and pray and seek my face, and turn from their wicked ways; then will I hear from heaven, and will forgive their sins, and will heal their land."

It's time to come out from among them and be ye separate. It's time to be clean and blood-washed redeemed folk. It's time that we follow Jesus and be not like them. Let the church be the church and let the world be the world. On this day, let's make our calling and election sure. Let's serve the Lord and let's serve the Lord with gladness.

Love,

JTJR

Stairway To Heaven, Step By Step

I say this with a smile on my face: the O'Jays aren't the only ones trying to make it to Heaven. Heaven is our goal. But there are steps to get there.

"And brought them out, and said, Sirs, what must I do to be saved? And they said, Believe on the Lord Jesus Christ, and thou shalt be saved, and thy house. And they spake unto him the word of the Lord, and to all that were in his house. And he took them the same hour of the night, and washed their stripes; and was baptized, he and all his, straightway." (Acts 16:30–33)

Just a little background on this text: Paul and Silas were on a mission preaching and teaching the Gospel of Jesus Christ. They were casting demons out, baptizing, healing—the whole nine yards. And there were some haters in the land that wanted to take them out. When we are doing the work of the Lord, we will run into some haters of Christ. There are some folk in your life right now that don't like you and they don't want to see you make it to that city called Heaven. The devil's job remains the same: kill, steal, and destroy.

Back to the text, in Acts Chapter 16, these anti-Christs went to the leaders and rulers of the land and told them that Paul and Silas were teaching customs that weren't lawful for them to receive, nor to observe. Then a multitude rose up against them; the rulers and leaders commanded that they be beaten. The Bible said that they received many stripes then they were cast into prison. There are some folk like that right now who don't want to hear the Gospel; they don't want to hear the truth. They don't want some "man or woman" to preach to them. So they are trying to 'X' Jesus out of everything. Our nation is in trouble because they trying to 'X' God out of it. During the Christmas season we see X-MAS, some try to 'X' Christ out, but The 'X' is actually indicating the Greek letter 'Chi,' which is short for the Greek meaning 'Christ.'

But the story goes on. They get beat down, because of the Gospel of Jesus Christ, just like many saints. But the next thing you know, Paul and Silas had a prayer and praise meeting, and not only did God release them out of jail, but those around them were also released. And those who were around, And those who were around Paul and Silas asked a question: "Sirs, what must I do to be saved?"

Please understand everything you go through for the Kingdom of God will be worth it all. For Heaven rejoices over one soul that repents! He that winneth a soul is wise. The hell we go through, the hate that we may experience will all make sense at the end.

They told them, "Believe on the Lord Jesus Christ, and thou shalt be saved, and thy house."

He that cometh to God must first believe that he is! But it doesn't stop at believing, and it doesn't stop at Romans 10:9, so let's keep reading.

"And they spake unto him the word of the Lord, and to all that were in his house. And he took them the same hour of the night, and washed their stripes; and was baptized, he and all his, straightway." (Acts 16:30–33)

Paul and Silas gave them the scriptures and told them step by step about salvation. So many people don't know what salvation is. They don't know the steps to salvation because we have preachers and teachers cutting corners, cheating the folk out of the truth. I'm so glad that we still have some Bible-believing churches around where we still go by the book. Paul and Silas were going by the book. The same Paul who wrote Romans 10:9 is the same Paul who spoke the Word of the Lord to them and to their household. That same night those who asked what they must do to be saved went down in Jesus' name! They were baptized in Jesus' name.

There are people who want to be saved; they want to have a stronger relationship with Christ; they want to go to Heaven, and it's our job to preach and teach them the scriptures step by step. I can hear Jesus and John the Baptist say, "Repent for the Kingdom of God is at Hand." I can hear Jesus say he that believeth and is baptized shall be saved. I can hear Jesus say, "Ye must be born again of the water and of the spirit." I can hear Jesus saying holiness without shall no man see the Lord. I can hear the Word of God through Paul say we are buried with Christ. I can hear Peter say repent and be baptized in the name of Jesus Christ for the remissions of sins and ye shall receive the gift of the Holy Ghost.

It's our job to know the steps to Heaven. Not only is it our job to know it, but we must tell it to somebody who asks. Don't just stop at Acts 16:31, don't just stop at Romans 10:9, but know the whole plan of salvation. No more cutting corners. Never be too busy that you can't lead somebody to salvation. Take your time with them, tarry with them and give them the steps to Heaven because we all want to go to Heaven!

Love,

JTJR

TAKE CARE OF YOUR TEMPLE

"What? know ye not that your body is the temple of the Holy Ghost which is in you, which ye have of God, and ye are not your own? For ye are bought with a price: therefore glorify God in your body, and in your spirit, which are God's."
(1 Corinthians 6:19–20)

Rebellion is running wild in our society. Many who don't want to be corrected when doing wrong usually say, "Which one of my bills are you paying?" Many feel that they are in control of their bodies and they can do what they want, but we really need to get back to reality. In the beginning God created the heavens and the earth. It was God who made us from the dust. It's in God we live, move, and have our being. It's God that wakes us up and allows our bodies to rest. We are living in a body that's been paid for by Christ Jesus himself. So before we get beside ourselves, we need to understand and respect our creator. We belong to God. But because of Satan and sin, we have strayed away from the truth. Some of us have forsaken God. We have even provoked God unto anger. Let's be real; we know better.

In verse 19 Paul hits us with a "What?"

If we can be honest, we all have said, "What," at the foolishness we have found ourselves in. Paul had to remind us that our bodies are the temple of the Holy Ghost! Our bodies are not made to get tattoos. Our bodies are not made to go sleep with everybody and everyone that isn't our husbands or wives. Our bodies aren't made to get drunk with wine and *drank*; let's be clear. Ha, ha. Our bodies aren't made to do ungodly things, but our bodies belong to the Lord.

Apostle Paul told us in Romans 12 that we must present our bodies as a sacrifices holy and acceptable unto Christ which is our reasonable service. We must do inventory. We must lay aside every weight and sin that easily beset us! We must clean our house. We must clean our temple by any means necessary! There are some habits we must get rid of. There are some places we don't need to go to anymore. There are some people that we don't need to text, call, and hang with anymore. There's some deadweight we must get rid of now before it gets rid of us. We must die daily to the flesh. Let us live in the spirit and not after the flesh!

We want to welcome the Lord in our temples. We need to repent, turn from our wicked ways, and walk in the way of holiness. When we are in Christ Jesus, when we are in his presence, there is fullness of joy. There is peace, there is love, and there is salvation. Where the spirit of the Lord is there is liberty!

Let's honor the Lord in the way we live and how we take care of our temples!

Love,

JTJR

Final Thoughts

This devotional has truly been inspired by God's Word. We know the thoughts he thinks towards us are of good and not of evil, but we must also have the sense of urgency that we are in the last seconds before the rapture takes place and there are souls that must be saved. "Knowing the Terror of the Lord we persuade men" (2 Corinthians 2:5a). The wages of sin is death, but the gift of God is eternal through our Lord and Savior Jesus Christ.

Acknowledgements

I'm grateful to God for my parents Mr. and Mrs. John and Erzel Thomas. My parents taught me the ways of righteousness and holy living. We truly lived by the scripture "as for me and my house we shall serve the Lord." It's a blessing because my parents weren't extreme; they most certainly gave us balance. It's also a double blessing by God because my parents are also pastors. The rumor is, Pastor Kids (PKs) the worst kids on the planet. Ha, ha. It's a myth; don't believe the hype. I just thank God for his grace and the blood of Jesus and I can proudly say, I am that I am by the grace of God. Amen and amen! :)

Being a pastor's kid has its perks, but I've also seen the struggle that I shy away from. Ministry and being a pastor after God's own heart is a risky job! It's not for everybody; it's only for those who God called and chose. To cover and to look out for the flock's lives is a task that I still can't fathom. I pray for pastors and leaders every day.

I remember having church in the living room of my parents' house. We grew a little bit in membership and we held service in an elementary school. Then my father was installed at a base chapel that went from 50 members to 300 in 3 months. When the base closed up, we went back to the school, membership went back down, and we even had church at the house again. The struggle was real. The things my parents and pastors had to endure were very real! It was tough but to see my parents/pastors continue on with the work of the ministry really blessed my soul! Till this day I serve my bishop, pastor, and the House of Prayer Reformation Church. I don't attend and serve because my parents are the leaders, but I go because Jesus is there and there is a work for me in the HOP Church. I've been offered to play drums and make good money at other churches, but I declined all because the Lord will supply all my needs; I'm staying in the HOP without charge! The House of Prayer is where I'm growing and being poured into.

I'm grateful that my dad exposed me to great Apostolic Fathers and Mothers of the faith. These listed all have blessed me in a major way: Bishop Noel Jones; Bishop T. D. Jakes; the late great Bishop Norman L. Wagner; Apostle Huie L. Rogers; Bishop Lambert Gates, Sr.; Apostle Henry B. Alexander; the late great Bishop Kenneth Moales; Dr. Carolyn Showell; Pastor Sheryl Brady; Bishop James Ross;

Bishop C. Shawn Tyson; Bishop Liston Page, Jr.; Elder David Hollis; and a host of other preachers and teachers of the faith who have had a major impact on my life. I'm grateful my dad exposed me to preachers outside of the apostolic oneness arena, because I most certainly learned so much from Bishop Larry D. Trotter, Bishop Paul S. Morton, Prophet Todd Hall, Dr. Jamal H. Bryant, Bishop Herman Murray, and the late great Bishop G. E. Patterson. Bishop Patterson was a giant in the body of Christ! I miss his preaching. These preachers have all upped my game and study to become a better student of the Word. But my favorite preacher is my father Bishop John Thomas, Sr. One of my personal favorite sermons he preached: "God Is Looking For a Champion." He rocked Ford Memorial Temple in Philadelphia, PA. Shout to Bishop Andrew Ford II.

I want to thank my family for always being a blessing in my life! I love each and everyone, including the ones who have gone on to be with the Lord. Thank you to my grandparents; uncles; aunts; cousins; sisters Tarron, Vernell, Myesha, and Brittany; my brothers-in-law Steven and Reggie; and all my nieces and nephews—I love y'all.

My bishop preached, "Keep me on point." I'm grateful for my friends, saved and unsaved. All who have kept me in line and on point. I'm grateful for

LaTanya Morgan-Diaz. From 2007 till now, she has blessed me in so many ways and she challenged me to be a better me. I love you forever! I'm grateful for my boys: my best friend Dave Black; G4; J Stew; Will Niqk; TJ Chambers (that dude always kept me in line!); Johnell; Reggie, aka the custodian—there's too many to name and I'm drawing a blank... Ha, ha. I'm shaking my head, but you know who you are!

Last but not least, Mr. and Mrs. Chris and Shanet Dennis! They have been a blessing since day one! If it wasn't for Chris pulling my card, this book would not have materialized. He sat me down before Monday night prayer and pushed me towards one of my dreams and goals in life! I love both of y'all!

Let's do it big GAB LIFE!

www.ingramcontent.com/pod-product-compliance
Lightning Source LLC
LaVergne TN
LVHW051237080426
835513LV00016B/1639